THE REMNANT BLUEPRINT

Rediscovering the Fear of the Lord
A Prophetic Cry to the End-Time Church

PETER LENGWE

ISBN:
Softcover: 978-1-972299-54-8
Hardback: 978-1-972299-55-5
eBook: 978-1-972299-53-1

For permission requests, visit and write to the publisher at:

Peter Lengwe | THE BREAD OF LIFE GLOBAL MINISTRIES

ABOUT THE AUTHOR

Peter Lengwe is a passionate servant of the Lord Jesus Christ, called and anointed to proclaim truth with power, purity, and boldness in this end-time generation. Born with a deep hunger for the Word of God, Peter's walk with the Lord has been shaped by seasons of intense refinement, persecution, spiritual warfare, and divine revelation—experiences God used to form in him a heart that trembles before His holiness.

Over the past decade, the Holy Spirit has led Peter through many churches, ministries, and spiritual environments—not to settle, but to observe, discern, and understand the true condition of the Body of Christ. Through betrayals, false accusations, rejection from leaders, and the jealousy of those intimidated by the anointing on his life, Peter learned firsthand the difference between religious Christianity and a life governed by the fear of the Lord.

These valleys of suffering forged an unshakable love for God and a burning burden for His Church.

Peter is the author of several prophetic and theological works, including IN THE BEGINNING THE HEAVENS AND THE EARTH AS

CREATED (2022), Pierced for Our Transgressions, and Mystery Babylon and World Beasts Unveiled—books dedicated to unveiling biblical truth, strengthening the faith of believers, and preparing the Church for the soon return of Jesus Christ.

His writing is marked by:

- deep reverence for Scripture,

- prophetic clarity,

- strong theological foundations,

- bold confrontation of compromise,

- a burden for holiness,

- and an unwavering call to repentance and purity.

Peter believes the greatest tragedy of the modern Church is the loss of the fear of the Lord—an absence that has opened the door to deception, worldliness, spiritual weakness, and dead religion. In obedience to the voice of God, he wrote THE REMNANT BLUEPRINT as a prophetic cry to awaken the end-time remnant, restore holiness to the Church, and call God's people back to trembling before His Majesty.

When he is not writing, Peter dedicates his time to prayer, studying the Scriptures, and encouraging believers to deepen their relationship with the Lord Jesus Christ. His life mission is simple yet uncompromising:

To restore the fear of God, the holiness of God, and the truth of God to the Church before the return of the King.

ACKNOWLEDGMENTS

To the Almighty God,

the Holy One of Israel,

the Ancient of Days,

the consuming fire whose fear endures forever—

this book exists because of You.

Your Spirit breathed it.

Your hand guided it.

Your burden birthed it.

All glory, honor, and reverence belong to You alone.

To the Lord Jesus Christ,

the King of kings and Lord of lords,

the Bridegroom who is returning soon—

thank You for saving me,

calling me,

shaping me,

breaking me,

refining me,

and entrusting me with this message for Your Church.

May Your name be exalted through every word.

To the Lord Jesus Christ,

the King of kings and Lord of lords,

the Bridegroom who is returning soon—

thank You for saving me,

calling me,

shaping me,

breaking me,

refining me,

and entrusting me with this message for Your Church.

May Your name be exalted through every word.

To the Holy Spirit,

the Spirit of wisdom,

the Spirit of truth,

the Spirit of holiness,

the Spirit of conviction,

the Spirit of burning,

and the Spirit of the fear of the Lord—

thank You for teaching me,

correcting me,

comforting me,

and filling me with Your fire.

To those who caused me pain,

those who rejected me,

those who wounded me,

those who slandered me,

and those who misunderstood me—

I thank you.

Your actions drove me deeper into God.

Your rejection pushed me into intimacy.

Your hostility refined my character.

Your betrayal strengthened my fear of the Lord.

Without those storms,

this book would not exist.

God used every hurt as a hammer

to forge the message in my spirit.

To the faithful few God sent into my life—

those who encouraged me,

prayed for me,

stood with me,

spoke life to me,

and believed in the calling upon my life—

I am deeply grateful.

Your love and support were a reminder

that God always preserves a remnant.

To every reader holding this book,

may the fire of God touch your heart as you read these pages.

May the Spirit of the fear of the Lord grip you,

sanctify you,

purify you,

and transform you.

May these words awaken something ancient,

something holy,

something eternal in you.

May you rise as part of God's end-time remnant—

fearless, pure, faithful, and ready for the return of the King.

To all those who will teach this message,

preach this message,

or carry this burden into churches, homes, and nations—

may the Lord strengthen you,

uphold you,

and pour His Spirit upon you without measure.

And finally,

to everyone who has walked with me on this journey,

whether through encouragement or trial—

I honor you,

and I bless you.

This book is more than pages and ink.

It is a cry.

A trumpet.

A warning.

A call to holiness.

A summons back to the fear of the Lord.

May God be glorified.

May His remnant be awakened.

May His Church be restored.

May His fear fill the earth once again.

Amen.

PREFACE

For ten years, the Lord has taken me through many churches—not to observe their programs, music, or structures, but to observe their hearts. And the most alarming thing the Holy Spirit showed me was this:

The fear of the Lord has been lost in His house.

Psalm 19:9 says:

> *"The fear of the Lord is clean, enduring forever."*

But in these last days, the Church has replaced clean fear with casual faith.

We have replaced reverence with relevance, holiness with hype, conviction with comfort, and truth with tolerance.

The Church—meant to be a holy assembly—has slowly become a religious organization. We have worship without trembling, sermons without repentance, altars without tears, leaders without integrity, saints without purity, and crowds without discipleship.

And the Lord kept asking me one burning question:

"Where is My fear in My Church?"

I have watched believers lift hands in worship while harboring jealousy, hatred, slander, envy, and secret sin. I have seen leaders more concerned with positions, titles, power, and influence than with holiness, humility, and truth. I have seen spiritual gifts celebrated while the Giver of the gifts is dishonored.

And I realized something terrifying:

Without the fear of the Lord, the Church is just a religion.

Without the fear of the Lord, there is no presence.

Without the fear of the Lord, there is no holiness.

Without the fear of the Lord, there is no revival.

This book is not written out of offense or bitterness.

It is written out of a burden.

A cry from the heart of God.

Because we are running out of time.

This is the final hour.

The Spirit is calling His people back to the fear of the Lord, the foundation of wisdom, the beginning of holiness, the birthplace of repentance, and the doorway to revival.

Psalm 19:9 reveals that the fear of God is clean—it purifies.

And it endures forever—it is eternal.

This book is a call to return to that eternal, purifying fear.

Before the trumpet sounds.

Before the King returns.

INTRODUCTION:
A LAST-DAYS CRY TO THE BODY OF CHRIST

The greatest crisis in the last-days Church is not persecution.

It is not a lack of money, buildings, or leadership.

It is not the rise of immorality in the world.

The greatest crisis in the last-days Church is this:

We want God's blessing without God's fear.

We want revival without repentance.

We want miracles without holiness.

We want breakthrough without obedience.

We want anointing without consecration.

We want His presence without His purity.

But the Bible is clear:

"The fear of the Lord is clean, enduring forever."
—Psalm 19:9

If the fear of the Lord is clean, then a Church without fear is unclean.

If the fear of the Lord endures forever, then a Church without fear will not endure.

God is calling His people back to the ancient path, the old foundation—the one that built Abraham, Moses, Joshua, David, Daniel, Peter, Paul, and even Jesus Himself, of whom it was written:

"His delight is in the fear of the Lord."
—Isaiah 11:3

If Jesus delighted in the fear of the Lord, how can His Church despise it?

This is a cry to the modern body of Christ:

Return to the fear of the Lord before it is too late.

Return to the fear of the Lord before the lampstand is removed.

Return to the fear of the Lord before the glory departs.

Return to the fear of the Lord before deception overtakes the world.

Return to the fear of the Lord before the Bridegroom comes.

Because we are living in the last moments of the final days.

And this book is a trumpet to awaken a sleeping Church.

TABLE OF CONTENTS

CHAPTER ONE:
WHAT IS THE FEAR OF
THE LORD?

Understanding the Clean, Enduring Fear That God Demands

Psalm 19:9 — "The fear of the Lord is clean, enduring forever…"

1. THE FEAR OF THE LORD — THE MOST MISUNDERSTOOD TRUTH IN THE CHURCH

If there is one doctrine that Satan has worked tirelessly to erase from the modern Church, it is the fear of the Lord. Not because it harms believers, but because it protects them. Not because it destroys revival, but because it births revival. Not because it creates distance from God, but because it keeps us close to God.

Psalm 19:9 tells us two eternal truths:

1. The fear of the Lord is clean.
    It purifies the heart, mind, motives, and walk of the believer.

2.   The fear of the Lord endures forever.
      It is unchanging, eternal, and required by God in every
      generation—Old Covenant and New Covenant.

The fear of the Lord is not an Old Testament relic.

It is a New Testament requirement for every true follower of Christ.

2. THE BIBLICAL MEANING OF THE FEAR OF THE LORD

The Bible uses two key words to describe fear:

Hebrew: Yir'ah

Meaning awe, reverence, honor, holy trembling,

and the deep awareness of God's holiness.

Greek: Phobos

Meaning to be in holy awe, to hold God in such reverence that it affects your lifestyle, choices, behavior, and attitude.

The fear of the Lord is not terror that drives you away from God.

It is holy trembling that draws you near to God.

It is not being scared of God.

It is being scared to live without Him.

It is not fear that God will hurt you.

It is fear that you might hurt Him.

The fear of the Lord is the inner posture that says:

"Lord, You are holy.

I honor You above everything.

I do not want to grieve You, dishonor You, or treat You as common."

This is the foundation of a life that pleases God.

3. HOW THE FEAR OF THE LORD WAS LOST IN THE CHURCH

The modern Church has slowly shifted from a holy altar to a comfortable auditorium.

From reverence to relaxation.

From conviction to motivation.

From Scripture to self-help.

From trembling to entertainment.

From holiness to hype.

What happened?

A. Preaching Stopped Confronting Sin

Many sermons today comfort the sinner instead of converting the sinner.

B. Worship Became Emotion Instead of Adoration

Goosebumps replaced brokenness.

C. Leaders Began Protecting Positions Instead of Purity

The stage became more important than the altar.

D. Christians Began Worshiping Gifts Over the Giver

Jealousy, envy, slander, gossip, and competition replaced unity, humility, and love.

E. The Church Stopped Talking About Judgment

But you cannot understand God's love without understanding His holiness.

F. The Holy Spirit Was Replaced with Human Talent

When the fear of God is gone, the flesh takes over.

This chapter is not written to condemn.

It is written to awaken.

God is calling His people back to the clean fear that He loves.

4. THE FEAR OF THE LORD IS THE BEGINNING OF WISDOM

Proverbs 9:10

"The fear of the Lord is the beginning of wisdom..."

There is no true wisdom without the fear of the Lord.

There is no discernment, no understanding, no spiritual maturity,

and no victory over sin without the fear of the Lord.

Everything in the Christian life begins with fear:

- Salvation

- Obedience

- Holiness

- Prayer

- Discernment

- Purity

- Love

- Faithfulness

- Worship

- Revival

The fear of the Lord is the foundation stone upon which every other truth stands.

Take away the foundation, and the whole building collapses.

5. THE FEAR OF THE LORD PRODUCES HOLY LIVING

When a believer walks in the fear of the Lord:

- Their words become pure

- Their thoughts become clean

- Their actions become righteous

- Their heart becomes tender

- Their walk becomes holy

The fear of the Lord makes sin repulsive, not attractive.

It makes holiness desirable, not burdensome.

It replaces:

- Pride with humility

- Jealousy with contentment

- Lust with purity

- Gossip with silence

- Anger with gentleness

- Hypocrisy with sincerity

- Casual Christianity with consecration

The fear of the Lord is the cure for everything plaguing the modern Church.

6. HOW TO RECEIVE THE FEAR OF THE LORD

The fear of the Lord is not something you create inside yourself.

It is something God gives.

Isaiah 11:2 says the fear of the Lord is a Spirit:

"The Spirit of the Lord...
the Spirit of knowledge and of the fear of the Lord."

You receive the fear of the Lord by:

1. Asking God for it
   (Psalm 86:11)

2. Reading Scripture with a humble heart
   The Word produces fear.

3. Beholding God's holiness
   (Isaiah 6)
   Revelation produces trembling.

4. Turning away from sin at once
   Every act of obedience strengthens holy fear.

5. Walking closely with the Holy Spirit
   He teaches reverence.

6. Keeping your heart pure
   Sin kills fear; purity increases it.

The fear of the Lord is a gift, a grace, and a guardrail.

7. WHY THE FEAR OF THE LORD ENDURES FOREVER

Psalm 19:9 is prophetic.

It tells us that even in eternity—

before the throne, on the new earth,

in the New Jerusalem—

the people of God will still walk in holy fear.

Why?

Because God's holiness never changes.

His purity never fades.

His glory never diminishes.

His nature never evolves.

If the fear of the Lord endures forever, then:

- We needed it in the Garden

- We need it in the Church

- And we will need it in the Kingdom to come

The fear of the Lord is eternal.

CLOSING PRAYER

Father, in the name of Jesus,

restore to me the clean, holy, purifying fear of the Lord.

Take away every casual attitude,

every sinful desire,

every unclean thought,

every prideful motive.

Give me a heart that trembles at Your Word.

Give me a spirit that honors Your holiness.

Make me a vessel of purity, humility, and obedience.

Teach me to love what You love and hate what You hate.

Let the fear of the Lord become the foundation of my life,

the anchor of my walk,

and the atmosphere of my heart.

In Jesus' name. Amen.

CHAPTER TWO: WHY THE FEAR OF GOD IS THE PRINCIPAL THING

The Foundation of Wisdom, Holiness, and Last-Days Survival

Psalm 19:9 — "The fear of the Lord is clean, enduring forever…"

1. THE FEAR OF THE LORD IS NOT OPTIONAL — IT IS ESSENTIAL

In the last days, many Christians want blessings without obedience, anointing without consecration, power without purity, and revival without repentance. But this is impossible.

Scripture makes it clear:

> *"The fear of the Lord is the beginning of wisdom."*
> *—Proverbs 9:10*

If fear is the beginning, everything built without it is:

- fragile

- shallow

- temporary

- corrupt

- and spiritually dangerous

This is why so many believers fall.

This is why so many churches crumble.

This is why so many ministries collapse.

They built without the principal thing.

You can have knowledge… but without fear, it becomes pride.

You can have gifts… but without fear, they lead to arrogance.

You can have position… but without fear, it leads to corruption.

You can have prophecy… but without fear, it becomes manipulation.

You can have worship… but without fear, it becomes entertainment.

The fear of the Lord is the root that sustains everything else.

2. THE FEAR OF THE LORD WAS THE FOUNDATION OF EVERY GODLY MAN

Every man and woman who walked with God—everyone—began with the fear of the Lord.

Abraham

God said,

> *"Now I know that you fear God." (Gen. 22:12)*

Not: Now I know you love Me.

Not: Now I know you trust Me.

But: Now I know you fear Me.

The fear of the Lord was Abraham's proof of covenant faithfulness.

Moses

The entire purpose of the Exodus was summarized in one sentence:

"God has come to test you, that His fear may be before you, so that you may not sin." (Exod. 20:20)

Joshua

Israel's victory in the Promised Land was tied to this command:

"Fear the Lord and serve Him in sincerity." (Josh. 24:14)

David

He wrote more about the fear of the Lord than any other figure in the Bible.

Solomon

The wisest man in history concluded:

"Let us hear the conclusion of the whole matter:

Fear God and keep His commandments." (Eccl. 12:13)

The conclusion of life… is fear.

Isaiah

When he saw the Lord, he trembled and cried:

"Woe is me!" (Isa. 6:5)

The fear of God birthed his prophetic calling.

Jesus Christ

Isaiah prophesied:

> *"His delight is in the fear of the Lord." (Isa. 11:3)*

If the Son of God Himself delighted in it, how can His Church reject it?

3. WITHOUT THE FEAR OF THE LORD, THE CHURCH CANNOT SURVIVE THE LAST DAYS

Jesus warned that in the last days:

- deception will increase

- false prophets will multiply

- sin will abound

- love will grow cold

- many will fall away

- the elect themselves will be tested

What is the one thing that protects a believer from deception?

Not intelligence.

Not emotion.

Not "positive thinking."

Not spiritual gifts.

Not church attendance.

The Bible reveals the answer:

"The fear of the Lord is the beginning of wisdom."

Wisdom is not intellectual.

It is spiritual.

It is protection.

A believer who fears God cannot be easily deceived.

Why? Because the fear of the Lord:

- exposes false teaching

- reveals counterfeit spirituality

- keeps the believer in holiness

- guards the heart from pride

- produces humility

- convicts of sin

- opens the ear to God

- shuts the door to Satan

This is why Psalm 19:9 says the fear of the Lord endures forever—

because it is the only posture that will carry us through the final hour.

4. THE FEAR OF THE LORD IS THE PRINCIPAL THING BECAUSE IT PRODUCES OBEDIENCE

Every command in Scripture flows from the fear of God.

Every act of disobedience flows from a lack of fear.

Adam sinned because the fear of the Lord was absent.

Cain murdered because the fear of the Lord was absent.

Israel rebelled in the wilderness because the fear of the Lord was absent.

Samson fell because the fear of the Lord was absent.

Saul lost the throne because the fear of the Lord was absent.

Ananias and Sapphira died because the fear of the Lord was absent.

Every fall in Scripture begins with:

"A lack of fear."

But every victory begins with:

"A heart that feared the Lord."

Obedience is not produced by:

- motivational Sermons

- emotional worship

- church programs

- talents

- conferences

- leadership training

Obedience flows from fear.

If the fear of the Lord is not present, obedience will never be sustained.

5. THE FEAR OF THE LORD IS THE PRINCIPAL THING BECAUSE IT PRODUCES HOLINESS

Holiness is not a personality.

Holiness is not strictness.

Holiness is not legalism.

Holiness is the atmosphere of God's presence being formed inside a believer.

And holiness cannot exist without fear.

2 Corinthians 7:1 teaches:

> *"Perfecting holiness in the fear of God."*

Holiness and fear are inseparable.

No fear = no holiness.

No holiness = no presence.

No presence = no revival.

No revival = no transformation.

This is why Satan attacks the fear of the Lord first.

If he can remove fear, he removes holiness.

If he removes holiness, he removes God's presence.

If he removes presence, he replaces it with religion.

And when religion replaces presence, the Church becomes powerless.

6. THE FEAR OF THE LORD IS THE PRINCIPAL THING BECAUSE IT PRODUCES TRUE WORSHIP

God is not moved by volume, emotion, or musical excellence.

He is moved by reverence.

Psalm 22:23 says:

> *"You who fear the Lord, praise Him!"*

Worship without fear is noise.

Worship with fear is incense.

This is why many churches have music but no presence.

Talent but no glory.

Emotion but no transformation.

The fear of God is what turns worship from entertainment into encounter.

7. THE FEAR OF THE LORD IS THE PRINCIPAL THING BECAUSE IT PRODUCES LOVE

Many Christians do not understand this:

The fear of the Lord is the root of true love for God.

Jesus said:

"If you love Me, keep My commandments." (John 14:15)

But you cannot keep His commandments without holy fear.

Fear guards love.

Fear purifies love.

Fear deepens love.

Fear makes you faithful.

Fear makes you loyal.

Fear makes you true.

The fear of the Lord makes your love sincere—not emotional, but sacrificial.

8. THE FEAR OF THE LORD IS THE PRINCIPAL THING BECAUSE IT OPENS THE TREASURY OF GOD

Psalm 25:14 declares:

"The secret of the Lord is with those who fear Him."

There is a realm of:

- revelation

- wisdom

- insight

- discernment

- prophetic clarity

- divine mysteries

- spiritual depth

…that only opens to those who fear the Lord.

God does not reveal His secrets to casual Christians.

He reveals them to trembling ones.

The fear of the Lord is the key to the deep things of God.

9. THE FEAR OF THE LORD IS THE PRINCIPAL THING BECAUSE IT WILL JUDGE US IN THE END

Paul writes:

"We must all appear before the judgment seat of Christ." (2 Cor. 5:10)

Then he adds:

Even Paul—filled with revelations, caught up to heaven, used by God—walked in the fear of the Lord because he knew one day he would stand before Jesus.

The fear of the Lord prepares us for that day

— the day when our works are tested by fire.

The fear of the Lord is the principal thing because the One we fear now is the One we will stand before later.

CLOSING PRAYER

Heavenly Father,

teach me to make the fear of the Lord the principal thing in my life.

Strip away every form of pride, shallowness, compromise, and false wisdom.

Let Your fear grip my heart, guide my steps, purify my motives,

and anchor me in these last days.

Give me wisdom that comes only from fearing You.

Give me holiness that flows from reverence.

Give me obedience born from trembling honor.

Prepare me now to stand before the judgment seat of Christ.

In Jesus' name. Amen.

CHAPTER THREE:
THE BENEFITS OF LIVING IN THE FEAR OF THE LORD

The Blessings, Protection, and Promises Reserved for the Reverent

Psalm 19:9 — "The fear of the Lord is clean, enduring forever…"

Most teachings in the modern Church focus on blessings—

but very few teach that the blessings of God have conditions.

And the primary condition revealed throughout Scripture is this:

The fear of the Lord.

There are blessings for faith.

There are blessings for obedience.

There are blessings for repentance.

But the deepest blessings—

the ones that shape a life, guard a soul, and draw the presence of God—

are reserved for those who fear Him.

In this chapter, we will explore the rich, powerful, life-changing benefits the Bible promises to those who walk in holy fear.

1. THE FEAR OF THE LORD BRINGS DIVINE WISDOM

Proverbs 9:10

"The fear of the Lord is the beginning of wisdom."

Wisdom is not intelligence.

Wisdom is not education.

Wisdom is not cleverness.

Wisdom is the mind of God given to a humble heart.

Without the fear of the Lord, a Christian can:

- pray but lack direction

- read the Bible but lack understanding

- serve God but lack discernment

- worship God but lack spiritual depth

But when the fear of the Lord enters a believer's life, their mind becomes aligned with God's mind. Their decisions become clearer. Their motives become purer. Their path becomes straighter. Their understanding becomes deeper.

Holy fear unlocks divine wisdom.

2. THE FEAR OF THE LORD BRINGS GOD'S INTIMATE FRIENDSHIP

Psalm 25:14

"The secret of the Lord is with those who fear Him…"

There are two categories of believers:

1.   Those who know God's acts

2.   Those who know God's ways

The first group sees what God does.

The second group understands His heart.

And that second group is made up only of those who fear Him.

The fear of the Lord brings you into God's inner circle.

You begin to hear what others cannot hear.

You begin to see what others cannot see.

You begin to discern what others cannot discern.

It is not gifts that give revelation.

It is fear.

Holy fear gives you access to God's secrets, whispers, warnings, and mysteries.

3. THE FEAR OF THE LORD BRINGS DIVINE PROTECTION

Psalm 34:7

One of the greatest promises for those who fear God is angelic protection.

This protection is not automatic.

It is reserved.

Reserved for who?

For those who fear Him.

When you walk in holy fear:

- God surrounds you

- God defends you

- God shields you

- God protects your home

- God protects your family

- God protects your mind

- God protects your path

Enemies may rise, but they cannot prevail.

Weapons may form, but they cannot prosper.

Attacks may come, but they cannot destroy.

Fear of the Lord = favor

Fear of the Lord = protection

Fear of the Lord = victory

4. THE FEAR OF THE LORD EXTENDS AND PRESERVES LIFE

Proverbs 10:27

"The fear of the Lord prolongs days…"

This is not poetic talk.

This is a literal spiritual law.

When a person fears the Lord:

- they avoid sin that destroys

- they walk in obedience that preserves

- they live with humility that protects

- they make wise decisions

- they flee danger

- they guard their heart

- they live clean, stable lives

- they stay within God's protective boundaries

Fear of the Lord = longer life

Sin = shortened life

The fear of the Lord preserves both your days and your destiny.

5. THE FEAR OF THE LORD BRINGS GOD'S PROVISION

Psalm 34:9

"Oh, fear the Lord, you His saints!

God is not promising luxury.

He is promising sufficiency.

Those who fear Him lack nothing:

- No lack in peace

- No lack in direction

- No lack in purpose

- No lack in spiritual food

- No lack in growth

- No lack in divine support

- No lack in God's presence

- No lack in protection

This scripture is not about money.

It is about God Himself being enough.

The fear of the Lord brings a life of contentment, not comparison.

Contentment is one of the greatest blessings of the last days.

6. THE FEAR OF THE LORD BRINGS PURITY AND CLEANLINESS OF HEART

Psalm 19:9

"The fear of the Lord is clean..."

The fear of God cleanses the heart:

- It kills pride

- It destroys lust

- It removes jealousy

- It uproots bitterness

- It silences gossip

- It crushes envy

- It defeats hypocrisy

- It purifies motives

- It aligns the heart with holiness

Where the fear of the Lord is present, sin loses its grip.

Temptation loses its power.

The flesh loses its authority.

The fear of the Lord is like spiritual bleach—

it purifies the heart until it resembles Christ.

7. THE FEAR OF THE LORD BRINGS GOD'S CONSTANT ATTENTION

Psalm 33:18

> *"The eye of the Lord is on those who fear Him…"*

There is no greater blessing than this.

When God's eye is on you:

- His guidance is with you

- His protection is around you

- His favor follows you

- His blessings pursue you

- His presence surrounds you

- His correction shapes you

- His peace guards you

A believer who fears the Lord never walks alone.

8. THE FEAR OF THE LORD BRINGS TRUE SPIRITUAL STABILITY

Isaiah 33:6

"...the fear of the Lord is His treasure."

In the last days, the world will shake.

Nations will shake.

Economies will shake.

Churches will shake.

Leaders will fall.

Believers will be tested.

Faith will be tried.

But God gives a promise:

The fear of the Lord becomes your stability.

- When others panic, you have peace

- When others are confused, you have clarity

- When others fall, you stand

- When others compromise, you remain faithful

- When others lose hope, you remain steadfast

The fear of the Lord is the anchor of a soul in a shaking world.

9. THE FEAR OF THE LORD BRINGS HONOR FROM GOD

Proverbs 22:4

> *"By humility and the fear of the Lord*
> *Are riches, honor, and life."*

True honor does not come from people—

it comes from God.

And God honors the one who fears Him.

This honor is not earthly fame.

It is spiritual weight, authority, and respect.

The believer who walks in holy fear carries:

- spiritual weight

- credibility

- influence

- authority

- effectiveness

- the fragrance of Christ

Honor follows fear.

10. THE GREATEST BENEFIT: THE FEAR OF THE LORD BRINGS THE PRESENCE OF GOD

God does not dwell where He is not honored.

Repeatedly, Scripture connects fear with presence.

Psalm 85:9

> *"His salvation is near those who fear Him…"*

Where there is fear, God draws near.

Where there is reverence, God rests.

Where there is trembling, God moves.

Where there is holiness, God manifests Himself.

The fear of the Lord brings:

- revival

- anointing

- breakthroughs

- miracles

- deliverance

- glory

- transformation

The greatest blessing of the fear of the Lord is God Himself.

CLOSING PRAYER (End of Chapter Three)

Lord Jesus,

open my eyes to the rich blessings You give

to those who walk in the fear of the Lord.

Let wisdom fill my mind,

let purity fill my heart,

let protection surround my life,

let provision follow my steps,

and let Your presence dwell in me continually.

Teach me to treasure holy fear as my greatest blessing

and to walk in it daily with humility and obedience.

In Your holy name, Amen.

CHAPTER FOUR:
THE REPERUSSIONS OF LIVING WITHOUT THE FEAR OF THE LORD

The Dangers, Judgments, and Consequences of a Fearless Church

Psalm 19:9 — "The fear of the Lord is clean, enduring forever…"

The absence of the fear of the Lord is not a small issue.

It is not a mild weakness.

It is not a momentary lapse.

It is spiritually fatal.

Because where the fear of God disappears, sin increases, deception deepens, pride rises, holiness dies, and the presence of God withdraws.

This chapter reveals what Scripture teaches about the frightening consequences of living, worshiping, serving, or leading without holy fear.

This is not written for condemnation—

but as a warning cry to the last-days Church.

1. WITHOUT THE FEAR OF THE LORD, SIN BECOMES NORMAL

Romans 3:18 describes the wicked in one sentence:

"There is no fear of God before their eyes."

When fear disappears, sin becomes:

- tolerated

- excused

- justified

- normalized

- celebrated

The fearless Christian becomes comfortable in areas they should be convicted in.

Soon:

- gossip feels harmless

- bitterness feels justified

- envy feels normal

- lust feels natural

- lying feels small

- compromise feels acceptable

- prayerlessness feels trivial

- disobedience feels minor

This is the first step toward spiritual destruction.

2. WITHOUT THE FEAR OF THE LORD, THE PRESENCE OF GOD WITHDRAWS

Psalm 85:9

"His salvation is near those who fear Him…"

If salvation is near the reverent,

then distance comes to the irreverent.

A church without fear may have:

- music

- crowds

- programs

- talent

- leadership

- excitement

- activity

…but no presence.

Ichabod (1 Samuel 4:21) becomes the spiritual reality—

"The glory has departed."

Without fear, the presence lifts.

And when the presence lifts, the Church becomes a shell, a performance, a religion, not a living body.

3. WITHOUT THE FEAR OF THE LORD, PRIDE TAKES OVER

Pride is the first fruit of a life that does not fear God.

Proverbs 8:13

"The fear of the Lord is to hate pride..."

Which means:

Where there is no fear of God, there is pride.

Pride leads to:

- stubbornness

- rebellion

- spiritual blindness

- self-righteousness

- unteachable hearts

- dishonor

- independence from God

- judgment toward others

- hypocrisy

When the fear of God leaves, a believer becomes their own god, their own guide, their own standard.

Pride kills destinies.

Pride destroys ministries.

Pride blinds leaders.

And its root is always the same:

a lack of fear.

4. WITHOUT THE FEAR OF THE LORD, JEALOUSY AND COMPETITION ENTER THE CHURCH

Where fear is absent, flesh is present.

A church without fear becomes:

- jealous of callings

- threatened by gifts

- intimidated by anointing

- competitive in ministry

- slanderous toward the innocent

- gossip-driven

- dishonorable

- divisive

This is what i personally witnessed,

Christians lifting hands in worship while harboring:

- hatred

- jealousy

- slander

- secret plots

- insecurity

- envy

- pride

- spiritual intimidation

All this flows from one root: no fear of God.

A church that does not fear God will fear each other.

A church that does not honor God will attack each other.

A church that does not tremble before God will tear one another down.

5. WITHOUT THE FEAR OF THE LORD, LEADERSHIP BECOMES CORRUPT

When spiritual leaders lose the fear of God:

- the pulpit becomes a stage

- the altar becomes a platform

- ministry becomes entertainment

- the Word becomes diluted

- worship becomes performance

- money becomes the motive

- power becomes the goal

- people become tools

- truth becomes adjustable

Every corrupt leader in Scripture began with a loss of fear:

- Saul: lost the kingdom

- Eli's sons: died at God's judgment

- Samson: lost his anointing

- Ahab: led Israel into idolatry

- Judas: betrayed the Lord

- Ananias & Sapphira: fell dead for lying to the Spirit

This is why James warns:

> *"Not many of you should become teachers…"*
> *(James 3:1)*

Because God judges leaders more strictly:

Those who represent Him must fear Him.

6. WITHOUT THE FEAR OF THE LORD, WORSHIP BECOMES EMPTY

Isaiah 29:13

> *"These people draw near with their lips…*
> *but their hearts are far from Me."*

When fear is missing, worship becomes:

- emotional

- musical

- talent-driven

- sensational

- shallow

- insincere

God does not accept worship from those who do not honor Him.

Worship without fear is noise, not incense.

Performance, not adoration.

Songs, not sacrifice.

7. WITHOUT THE FEAR OF THE LORD, PRAYER BECOMES POWERLESS

Hebrews 5:7 reveals something powerful about Jesus:

"…He was heard because of His godly fear."

If Jesus Himself was heard because of fear,

how much more must we walk in it?

A believer without fear:

- prays casually

- prays without faith

- prays without focus

- prays without holiness

- prays without authority

The fear of the Lord is what gives prayer its weight, authority, and effectiveness.

8. WITHOUT THE FEAR OF THE LORD, FAMILY AND PERSONAL LIFE CRUMBLE

A life without fear will always drift into:

- compromise

- double-living

- secret sin

- impurity

- instability

- restlessness

- confusion

- spiritual blindness

Marriages suffer, children rebel, homes lose peace, and the spiritual foundation collapses. A home without fear becomes a playground for the enemy.

9. WITHOUT THE FEAR OF THE LORD, A BELIEVER FALLS INTO DECEPTION

1 Timothy 4:1

> *"In the last days, many will depart from the faith…"*

Why?

Because they lost fear.

The fear of the Lord:

- exposes false doctrine

- reveals spiritual danger

- protects from seducing spirits

- warns the conscience

- keeps the heart humble

- keeps the believer in truth

A believer who lacks fear becomes vulnerable to:

- false prophets

- charismatic manipulators

- deceptive doctrines

- emotional spirituality

- counterfeit anointing

- demonic influence

A fearless Christian is easily deceived.

A reverent Christian is spiritually unshakeable.

10. THE MOST TERRIFYING CONSEQUENCE: GOD WILL JUDGE THOSE WHO DO NOT FEAR HIM

Hebrews 10:31

"It is a fearful thing to fall into the hands of the living God."

Final judgment is not the problem.

Living without fear is the problem.

Romans 2:5 speaks of those who live without fear:

"You are treasuring up wrath for the day of wrath…"

Every sin ignored, every compromise accepted,

every warning rejected,

every conviction silenced

is recorded.

Peter writes:

> *"Judgment must begin in the house of God."*
> *(1 Peter 4:17)*

God will judge:

- pastors who lost fear

- leaders who abused power

- churches that compromised

- Christians who dishonored Him

- worshipers who sang without holiness

- prophets who prophesied without truth

- believers who lived without repentance

This is not to condemn—

but to wake us up.

We are running out of time.

CLOSING PRAYER

Father,

open my eyes to the dangers of living without Your holy fear.

Do not allow pride, compromise, deception, or sin to find a home in me.

Remove every casual attitude toward Your presence,

every hidden sin,

40

every impure motive,

and every trace of spiritual laziness.

Restore to me the trembling reverence that protects, guides, and purifies.

Let the fear of the Lord anchor my heart and guard my walk.

In Jesus' mighty name, Amen.

CHAPTER FIVE: HOW GOD COMMANDS US TO LIVE IN THE FEAR OF THE LORD

Returning to Reverence, Walking in Obedience, and Guarding Holy Fear Daily

Psalm 19:9 — "The fear of the Lord is clean, enduring forever…"

God does not simply suggest that we fear Him.

He commands it.

From Genesis to Revelation, the fear of the Lord is the lifestyle required of every believer—especially in the last days.

Living in the fear of the Lord is not accidental.

It is intentional.

It is pursued.

It is cultivated.

It is protected.

This chapter reveals how God Himself instructs us to walk in holy fear every day of our lives.

1. GOD COMMANDS HIS PEOPLE TO FEAR HIM

Psalm 33:8

"Let all the earth fear the Lord; let all the inhabitants of the world stand in awe of Him."

This command is universal:

- all nations

- all believers

- all leaders

- all ages

- all generations

Fear of God is not outdated.

It is not Old Testament.

It is not optional.

It is the command that makes all other commands possible.

Without the fear of the Lord, obedience collapses.

2. GOD COMMANDS US TO FEAR HIM FOR OUR OWN GOOD

Deuteronomy 10:12–13

"What does the Lord require of you…
but to fear the Lord your God…
for your good?"

God commands fear not for His benefit—

but for ours.

Why?

Because holy fear:

- protects you

- purifies you

- guides you

- anchors you

- strengthens you

- humbles you

- disciplines you

- preserves you

- keeps you from sin

- keeps you in truth

Fear of the Lord is divine safety.

3. GOD COMMANDS US TO WALK IN FEAR DAILY

Psalm 128:1

> *"Blessed is everyone who fears the Lord,*
> *and walks in His ways."*

Fear is not an emotion.

It is a walk.

A lifestyle.

A daily posture.

A continuous obedience.

You cannot fear God on Sunday and forget Him on Monday.

You cannot fear Him in worship and ignore Him in private.

You cannot fear Him in church and dishonor Him at home.

Fear is a walk—

a long journey of daily surrender.

4. GOD COMMANDS US TO FEAR HIM IN SECRET

Matthew 6 reveals a powerful truth:

The Father who sees in secret rewards openly.

True fear of the Lord begins where:

- no crowd sees

- no church watches

- no leader hears

- no audience is present

- no applause can be earned

Fear of God is measured in the secret life,

where motives, thoughts, desires, and habits live.

A man who fears God in secret will never fall in public.

A woman who honors God in private will never be disgraced in ministry.

Fear begins in the hidden place.

5. GOD COMMANDS US TO FEAR HIM IN THE WORD

Isaiah 66:2

> *"...to this one I will look:*
> *the one who is humble,*
> *and who trembles at My Word."*

The fear of the Lord is impossible without the Word of God.

When the Word becomes:

- optional

- negotiable

- occasional

- inconvenient

- flexible

- adjustable

...fear disappears.

But when the Word is:

- obeyed

- honored

- loved

- trembled at

- meditated on

- submitted to

…fear grows.

To walk in holy fear, you must let Scripture judge you rather than you judging Scripture.

6. GOD COMMANDS US TO FEAR HIM IN HOLINESS

2 Corinthians 7:1

"…perfecting holiness in the fear of God."

Fear produces holiness.

Holiness deepens fear.

They are inseparable.

If you stop pursuing holiness,

you will stop fearing God.

If you stop fearing God,

you will stop pursuing holiness.

Holiness is not legalism.

Holiness is love expressed through obedience.

To fear God is to hate sin.

To fear God is to avoid every appearance of evil.

To fear God is to flee temptation, not flirt with it.

7. GOD COMMANDS US TO FEAR HIM THROUGH OBEDIENCE

Ecclesiastes 12:13

"Fear God and keep His commandments..."

How do you prove you fear Him?

Not by singing.

Not by emotions.

Not by tears.

Not by words.

Obedience is the evidence.

A believer who truly fears God says:

- "Yes, Lord."

- "Your way, not mine."

- "Your will, not mine."

- "Your Word, not my feelings."

Fear produces submission.

Submission produces obedience.

Obedience produces blessing.

8. GOD COMMANDS US TO FEAR HIM BY CHOOSING WISE FRIENDSHIPS

Proverbs 13:20

"He who walks with wise men will be wise..."

Why do many Christians lose the fear of the Lord?

Because they walk with people who fear nothing.

If you surround yourself with:

- gossipers

- lukewarm believers

- carnal friends

- compromising Christians

- rebellious spirits

...your fear of God will slowly die.

Community must protect fear.

If you want to fear God, you must walk with those who tremble before Him.

9. GOD COMMANDS US TO FEAR HIM THROUGH HUMILITY

Proverbs 22:4

"By humility and the fear of the Lord..."

Fear cannot grow in a proud heart.

Humility:

- admits weakness

- confesses sin

- seeks correction

- welcomes accountability

- submits to counsel

- recognizes God's authority

Fear grows where humility lives.

Pride kills fear.

Humility cultivates fear.

10. GOD COMMANDS US TO FEAR HIM IN THE LAST DAYS

Jesus warned that in the end times:

- lawlessness will abound

- deception will increase

- love will grow cold

- false doctrine will flourish

- holiness will be mocked

- many will fall away

What is the antidote?

The fear of the Lord.

The early Church walked in it:

Acts 9:31

"...walking in the fear of the Lord and in the comfort of the Holy Spirit..."

Fear and the Holy Spirit go together.

Fear protects you from deception.

Fear keeps you steady.

Fear preserves your love for God.

Fear strengthens your holiness.

Fear prepares you for Christ's return.

The fear of the Lord will carry the Church through the final hour.

CLOSING PRAYER (End of Chapter Five)

Father,

teach me to walk in the fear of the Lord every day of my life.

Help me to honor You in secret and in public,

in the Word and in prayer,

in holiness and obedience,

in motives and decisions.

Surround me with people who fear You,

purify my heart from every prideful thought,

and keep me humble, trembling, and faithful.

Make the fear of the Lord my lifestyle,

my anchor, and my protection.

In Jesus' name. Amen.

CHAPTER SIX: EXAMPLES OF THE FEAR OF THE LORD IN SCRIPTURE

Men and Women Who Walked in Holy Fear and Carried the Presence of God

Psalm 19:9 — "The fear of the Lord is clean, enduring forever..."

God never calls His people to walk in something they have not seen demonstrated.

Throughout the Bible, men and women who carried the fear of the Lord also carried:

- divine favor

- supernatural protection

- prophetic revelation

- wisdom beyond their time

- courage under pressure

- purity of heart

- the presence of God

The fear of the Lord is not an abstract idea—it is a lifestyle revealed in the lives of the faithful.

Let us look at some of the most striking biblical examples.

1. ABRAHAM — THE FATHER OF FAITH WHO FEARED GOD FIRST

Genesis 22:12

"Now I know that you fear God..."

God did not say:

- "Now I know you love Me."

- "Now I know you trust Me."

- "Now I know you are faithful."

He said: "Now I know you fear Me."

The fear of God was Abraham's proof of covenant loyalty.

What Abraham teaches us:

- Fear = obedience even when you don't understand

- Fear = surrendering the most precious thing

- Fear = trusting God more than anything else

- Fear = worship with sacrifice

Abraham's entire destiny was confirmed by fear.

2. JOSEPH — THE MAN WHO FLED SIN BECAUSE HE FEARED GOD

Genesis 39:9

"How then can I do this great wickedness, and sin against God?"

Joseph did not fear Potiphar.

He feared the Lord.

And that fear empowered him to run from temptation.

What Joseph teaches us:

- Fear = purity when no one is watching

- Fear = integrity in secret

- Fear = refusing sin at any cost

- Fear = divine protection

- Fear = favor that lifts you from prison to palace

His fear of God preserved his destiny.

3. MOSES — THE LEADER WHO FEARED GOD ABOVE PEOPLE

Hebrews 11:27

"He endured as seeing Him who is invisible."

Moses feared God more than Pharaoh, more than Israel, more than pressure, and more than the future.

What Moses teaches us:

- Fear of God > fear of people

- Fear empowers courage

- Fear preserves leadership integrity

- Fear leads to encounters with God

- Fear gives authority

Moses became great because he feared the One who called him.

4. THE HEBREW MIDWIVES — WOMEN WHO FEARED GOD AND SAVED A NATION

Exodus 1:17

> *"But the midwives feared God, and did not do as the king commanded..."*

They defied Pharaoh—a global superpower—because they feared God more.

What the midwives teach us:

- Fear produces boldness in women of God

- Fear values life

- Fear stands against evil

- Fear brings divine blessing

God rewarded them with households and legacy because of their fear.

5. JOSHUA — THE WARRIOR WHO SERVED GOD WITH REVERENCE

Joshua 24:14

"Now therefore, fear the Lord, serve Him in sincerity and truth..."

Joshua lived in holy fear and led Israel to victory.

What Joshua teaches us:

- Fear leads to spiritual leadership

- Fear produces courage

- Fear keeps you loyal

- Fear brings generational blessing

Joshua's fear of God made him undefeatable.

6. RAHAB — A GENTILE WOMAN WHO FEARED GOD ABOVE HER PEOPLE

Joshua 2:11

"Our hearts melted... for the Lord your God, He is God in heaven and on earth."

Rahab feared God before she ever knew Him.

What Rahab teaches us:

- Fear of God draws even outsiders

- Fear produces repentance

- Fear leads to salvation

- Fear brings redemption

- Fear brings inclusion in God's plan

Rahab went from harlot to hero—because she feared the Lord.

7. DAVID — THE MAN WHO TREMBLED AT GOD'S HOLINESS

Psalm 34:11

"Come, children, listen to me; I will teach you the fear of the Lord."

David experienced the consequences of irreverence when Uzzah touched the Ark.

1 Chronicles 13:12

"David was afraid of God that day..."

And that fear became the foundation of his leadership.

What David teaches us:

- Fear makes you careful with holy things

- Fear leads to repentance

- Fear softens the heart

- Fear draws God's presence

David's fear of God shaped his entire reign.

8. JOB — THE MAN WHO FEARED GOD AND TURNED FROM EVIL

Job 1:1

"...that man was blameless... one who feared God and shunned evil."

God Himself testified of Job's fear.

What Job teaches us:

- Fear produces holiness

- Fear produces integrity

- Fear withstands trials

- Fear attracts God's attention

- Fear silences Satan

Job's fear gave him spiritual authority.

9. DANIEL — THE MAN WHO WOULD NOT COMPROMISE

Daniel 1:8

"Daniel purposed in his heart... "

He feared God more than Babylon, culture, kings, or lions.

What Daniel teaches us:

- Fear produces unshakeable conviction

- Fear produces spiritual excellence

- Fear brings divine revelation

- Fear gives supernatural protection

- Fear elevates you in dark places

Daniel's fear made him a prophet and a statesman.

10. HANANIAH, MISHAEL & AZARIAH — THE MEN WHO FEARED GOD ABOVE FIRE

Daniel 3:16

"We do not need to defend ourselves... our God is able... "

Their reverence made them fearless.

What they teach us:

- Fear of God produces courage against threats

- Fear produces loyalty unto death

- Fear invites supernatural intervention

- Fear brings Christ into the fire

They feared God and God delivered them from fire.

11. MARY — THE WOMAN WHO FEARED GOD AND FOUND FAVOR

Luke 1:50

"His mercy is on those who fear Him from generation to generation."

Mary was chosen because she feared God.

What Mary teaches us:

- Fear prepares the heart for divine assignment

- Fear produces purity

- Fear births humility

- Fear brings generational blessing

The fear of the Lord positioned Mary for destiny.

12. CORNELIUS — A GENTILE WHO FEARED GOD AND OPENED THE DOOR TO THE NATIONS

Acts 10:2

"...a devout man and one who feared God..."

God sent an angel to Cornelius and used him to open the Gospel to the Gentile world.

What Cornelius teaches us:

- Fear draws heaven's attention

- Fear brings divine visitation

- Fear opens spiritual doors

- Fear leads to household salvation

Fear of the Lord leads to powerful spiritual breakthrough.

13. JESUS CHRIST — THE SON OF GOD WHO DELIGHTED IN THE FEAR OF THE LORD

Isaiah 11:2–3

"...the Spirit of the fear of the Lord... and His delight is in the fear of the Lord."

Even Jesus—sinless, perfect, divine—walked in holy fear.

What Jesus teaches us:

- Fear of God is not for the weak

- Fear is not legalism

- Fear is not Old Covenant

- Fear is the lifestyle of the purest Man who ever lived

If Jesus delighted in fear, then the Church must return to it.

REFLECTION

These men and women did not fear God because they were strong.

They feared God because they were surrendered.

And because they feared Him:

- they walked in purity

- they walked in revelation

- they walked in authority

- they walked in favor

- they walked in protection

- they walked in power

- they walked in purpose

- they walked in intimacy

Wherever the fear of the Lord is present, the presence of the Lord is near.

CLOSING PRAYER

Father,

thank You for the examples of men and women

who walked in the fear of the Lord

and carried Your glory with honor.

Help me to follow them.

Give me the purity of Joseph,

the courage of Daniel,

the reverence of David,

the obedience of Abraham,

the humility of Mary,

and the faithfulness of Jesus Himself.

Let their lives be my blueprint

and let Your holy fear be my foundation.

In Jesus' mighty name, Amen.

62

CHAPTER SEVEN:
THE SPIRIT OF RELIGION:
THE ABSENCE OF THE
FEAR OF THE LORD

How Religion Replaces Reverence, Blocks Revival, and Seeks Its Own Way

Psalm 19:9 — "The fear of the Lord is clean, enduring forever…"

1. THE SPIRIT OF RELIGION IS THE OPPOSITE OF THE FEAR OF THE LORD

Where the fear of the Lord produces humility, holiness, repentance, and surrender—

the spirit of religion produces:

- pride

- hypocrisy

- self-righteousness

- rebellion

- empty worship

- counterfeit spirituality

- jealousy and competition

- man-made traditions

- false appearances of holiness

Religion is what you get when:

the form of godliness replaces the fear of God.

Paul described this perfectly:

> *"...having a form of godliness but denying its power."*
> —2 Timothy 3:5

Religion has a form—

but not the fear.

A look—

but not the life.

A sound—

but not the substance.

Religion performs for people;

fear of God lives before the Lord.

2. RELIGION SEEKS ITS OWN WAY — NOT GOD'S WAY

Isaiah 58:2 describes religious people with chilling accuracy:

*"They seek Me daily… they delight to know My ways…
but they do not forsake their sins."*

Religion wants:

- worship without holiness

- Scripture without submission

- prayer without repentance

- ministry without sacrifice

- positions without purity

- blessings without obedience

- anointing without surrender

Religion seeks God —

but only on its own terms.

True fear of the Lord says:

"Not my will, but Yours be done."

Religion says:

"Not Your will—mine be done."

This is why the spirit of religion is so dangerous:

it pretends to serve God but serves self.

3. RELIGION PRODUCES BEHAVIOR WITHOUT TRANSFORMATION

Jesus confronted religion more than demons.

Why? Because religious people always look holy—

but lack the fear that transforms the heart.

Matthew 23:27

"You are like whitewashed tombs… beautiful outwardly, but inside full of dead men's bones…"

Religion focuses on:

*   outward behavior

*   outward appearance

*   outward performance

*   outward holiness

But the heart stays:

*   unchanged

*   unrepentant

*   unbroken

*   unsubmitted

*   unclean

True fear of the Lord cleans the inside first.

Religion cleans the outside only.

4. RELIGION BREEDS HYPOCRISY BECAUSE IT HAS NO FEAR

The Pharisees prayed, fasted, tithed, memorized Scripture—

but Jesus said they were:

- blind guides

- hypocrites

- fools

- spiritually dead

Why?

Because they lacked the fear of the Lord.

Religion produces:

- jealousy of others' gifts

- envy of others' anointing

- slander against the innocent

- secret hatred

- competition

- backbiting

- division

This is exactly what I personally witnessed:

Christians raising hands in worship while harboring hatred in their hearts.

This is not a prayer issue—

it is a fear issue.

5. RELIGION HONORS GOD WITH LIPS BUT NOT WITH LIFE

Isaiah 29:13

"This people draw near with their mouth...
but their heart is far from Me,
and their fear toward Me is taught by the commandments of men."

Religion replaces true fear with:

- man's opinions

- man's teachings

- man's traditions

- man's ideas

- man's standards

Men teach religious fear.

The Spirit teaches true fear.

Jesus said that religious people honor Him with lips—

but their hearts are far away.

Religion loves performance.

The fear of the Lord loves presence.

6. RELIGION DESTROYS LOVE BECAUSE IT DESTROYS FEAR

Where there is no fear of God,

there is no love for people.

A religious person will:

- gossip about a brother

- compete with a sister

- slander an innocent servant

- scheme against a humble believer

- envy a gifted minister

- mistreat a righteous person

Why?

Because they fear men, not God.

They fear losing position, not losing purity.

They fear losing influence, not losing holiness.

Religion destroys love because it destroys fear—

and without the fear of the Lord, sin grows in the heart.

7. RELIGION PERSECUTES THOSE WHO CARRY TRUE FEAR

Throughout Scripture:

- Joseph's purity provoked hatred

- Moses' obedience provoked resistance

- David's anointing provoked jealousy

- Jeremiah's messages provoked persecution

- Daniel's holiness provoked plots

- Jesus' purity provoked crucifixion

Why?

Because the spirit of religion cannot tolerate those who walk in true fear of the Lord.

When you fear God:

- your presence convicts the religious

- your purity exposes their hypocrisy

- your humility reveals their pride

- your reverence exposes their irreverence

- your anointing exposes their emptiness

Religion always attacks the righteous.

8. RELIGION HAS POWER WITHOUT PRESENCE

Like Samson after his fall, religion "shakes itself,"

tries to perform,

tries to imitate anointing…

…but God has left the building.

Revelation 3:1

"You have a name that you are alive, but you are dead."

People think the church is alive.

God says it is dead.

Why?

Because the fear of the Lord is gone.

Religion has:

- crowds but no glory

- music but no presence

- sermons but no conviction

- activity but no transformation

- gifts but no holiness

- titles but no humility

- noise but no power

Fearlessness = presence-less Christianity.

9. RELIGION ALWAYS LEADS TO JUDGMENT

Hebrews 10:31

"It is a fearful thing to fall into the hands of the living God."

When fear is gone:

judgment begins

lampstands are removed

glory departs

deception increases

leaders fall

churches die

believers drift

sin multiplies

God judges religion more harshly than immorality—

because religion pretends to represent Him while dishonoring Him.

Jesus cleansed the temple—

not the brothel.

Because religion pollutes God's house.

10. A CHURCH WITHOUT FEAR BECOMES A RELIGION — NOT A BRIDE

The Bride fears the Bridegroom.

Religion fears losing control.

The Bride seeks His face.

Religion seeks position.

The Bride seeks holiness.

Religion seeks attention.

The Bride seeks obedience.

Religion seeks performance.

The Bride seeks intimacy.

Religion seeks influence.

The fear of the Lord separates the Bride from the religious crowd.

CLOSING PRAYER (End of Chapter Seven)

Father,

deliver me from every spirit of religion.

Set me free from empty traditions,

self-righteousness,

jealousy,

pride,

competition,

and hypocrisy.

Destroy every form of godliness that denies Your power.

Restore in me true fear—

the fear that produces holiness,

love,

humility,

and obedience.

Make me a child of Your presence,

not a slave of religion.

In Jesus' mighty name, Amen.

CHAPTER EIGHT:
THE FEAR OF THE LORD:
THE GATEWAY TO
INTIMACY WITH GOD

How Holy Reverence Leads to Union, Communion, and Spiritual Intercourse with the Almighty

Psalm 19:9 — "The fear of the Lord is clean, enduring forever…"

There is a level of relationship with God that many Christians never experience—

a realm beyond blessings, beyond answered prayer, beyond spiritual gifts.

It is the realm of:

- union

- communion

- fellowship

- revelation

- divine nearness

- spiritual oneness

- heart-to-heart intimacy with God

This realm is only available to those who fear the Lord.

1. FEAR OF THE LORD IS THE DOORWAY TO GOD'S INNER COURT

Psalm 25:14

> *"The secret of the Lord is with those who fear Him..."*

The word "secret" in Hebrew (sowd) means:

- intimate conversation

- heart-to-heart counsel

- confidential whispers

- divine secrets shared in friendship

- the private chamber of the King

Fear gives access.

Not everyone is invited into God's inner chamber.

Not everyone hears God's whispers.

Not everyone knows His secrets.

Gifts may take you into ministry.

Only fear takes you into intimacy.

2. FEAR OF THE LORD LEADS TO SPIRITUAL UNION WITH GOD

1 Corinthians 6:17

"He who is joined to the Lord is one spirit with Him."

This "joining" is spiritual union—

the deepest level of relationship with God a believer can experience.

But union requires cleanness.

Psalm 19:9 says:

"The fear of the Lord is clean..."

Fear purifies the heart so deeply

that the Holy Spirit has no resistance, no blockage, no hindrance in the believer.

Fear prepares the heart for union.

3. FEAR OF THE LORD IS THE FOUNDATION OF FRIENDSHIP WITH GOD

Consider Abraham:

Isaiah 41:8

"...Abraham My friend..."

Why was Abraham called God's friend?

Because God said:

"Now I know that you fear Me."
—Genesis 22:12

Friendship with God is the fruit of fear.

Without fear, intimacy is impossible.

Religion may know God's name.

Only the reverent know His heart.

4. FEAR OF THE LORD PRODUCES HOLY VULNERABILITY

Intimacy requires:

- openness

- transparency

- honesty

- brokenness

- vulnerability

But fear of the Lord makes this possible.

Isaiah 66:2

> *"...to him who is humble and contrite in spirit,
> and who trembles at My word."*

Fear strips away pride.

Fear crushes self-will.

Fear breaks hardness of heart.

Fear creates spiritual tenderness.

You cannot be intimate with God if pride remains.

Fear removes the barriers.

5. FEAR OF THE LORD BRINGS GOD TO REVEAL HIS HEART

John 15:15

*"No longer do I call you servants…
but friends, for all things I heard from My Father I have made
known to you."*

Servants obey.

Friends receive disclosure.

God reveals secrets only to those who fear Him.

This is "intercourse" with God—not physical, but spiritual:

the exchange of deep things, the planting of divine truth, the imparting of revelation.

Just as a husband plants seed into a wife's womb,

so, God plants revelation into the womb of the spirit.

And FEAR is the doorway.

6. FEAR OF THE LORD MAKES YOU A DWELLING PLACE FOR GOD

John 14:23

*"If anyone loves Me… My Father will love him,
and We will come to him and make Our home with him."*

Love produces obedience.

Obedience flows from fear.

Fear prepares the "house" of your heart

for God to live, breathe, and dwell.

Fear makes you:

- a resting place

- a home

- a sanctuary

- a habitation of God

This is intimacy at its highest.

7. FEAR OF THE LORD CREATES INSIDE YOU A PLACE FOR GOD'S SEED

1 John 3:9

"...His seed remains in him..."

This "seed" (sperma) stands for:

- divine truth

- revelation

- the Word

- spiritual life

- God's nature

- God's character

Fear makes the heart:

- open

- receptive

- fertile

- submissive

- obedient

Fear is the preparation for divine conception.

Without fear, the seed cannot remain.

Without fear, revelation is aborted.

Without fear, intimacy is blocked.

8. FEAR OF THE LORD GIVES YOU ACCESS TO GOD'S PRESENCE

Psalm 31:19–20

"How great is Your goodness...
which You have prepared for those who fear You!
You shall hide them in the secret place of Your presence..."

There is a place called:

- the secret place

- the inner chamber

- the holy of holies

- the place of union

- the place where God reveals His glory

Fear is the entrance key.

Many Christians desire God's presence…

but only those who fear Him live in it.

9. FEAR OF THE LORD MAKES INTIMACY SAFE

God is holy.

God is pure.

God is consuming fire.

Intimacy with Him without fear is dangerous.

Hebrews 12:28

> *"...serve God acceptably*
> *with reverence and godly fear..."*

Without fear, intimacy turns into:

- entitlement

- disrespect

- casualness

- irreverence

- pride

- spiritual immaturity

Fear protects the relationship.

Fear keeps intimacy holy.

Fear ensures we approach God with:

- reverence

- brokenness

- humility

- purity

10. FEAR OF THE LORD LEADS TO REVELATION INTERCOURSE

In the literal sense, intercourse means:

- exchange

- impartation

- union

- conception

- fruitfulness

Spiritually, the fear of the Lord leads to the same:

A. Exchange

Your will for His will.

Your desires for His desires.

B. Impartation

God deposits His Word, His thoughts, His wisdom, His revelation.

C. Union

Your spirit becomes one with His Spirit (1 Cor. 6:17).

D. Conception

New revelation, new anointing, new assignments are conceived within you.

E. Fruitfulness

Your life produces holiness, obedience, and spiritual maturity.

Fear of the Lord is the marriage covenant of the spirit

that allows God to plant His nature inside you.

CLOSING PRAYER (End of Chapter Eight)

Holy Father,

take me deeper into intimacy with You.

Remove every hardness,

every pride,

every barrier,

every distraction

that blocks true communion with You.

Teach me to tremble at Your Word.

Prepare my heart as a holy place for Your presence.

Let Your fear purify me

so Your Spirit can dwell in me without hindrance.

Join my spirit to Yours,

conceive Your truth within me,

and make me one with You in purpose,

In desire,

and in holiness.

In Jesus' holy name. Amen.

**CHAPTER NINE:
THE FEAR OF THE LORD:
THE SPIRITUAL WOMB
WHERE GOD BIRTHS HIS
NATURE, HIS WORD, AND
HIS GLORY IN US**

The Mysteries of Divine Conception, Spiritual Pregnancy, and God's Indwelling Life

Psalm 19:9 — "The fear of the Lord is clean, enduring forever…"

The fear of the Lord does not merely produce intimacy.

Intimacy is the gateway.

Fear is the environment.

Fear is the atmosphere.

Fear is the womb.

Fear is the holy chamber.

Fear is the inner sanctuary where God plants Himself inside a believer.

Every man and woman God ever used became a spiritual womb—

but only after they walked in holy fear.

Let's go deeper.

1. THE FEAR OF THE LORD CREATES A SPIRITUAL WOMB INSIDE THE BELIEVER

Psalm 51:6

"You desire truth in the inward parts…"

"Inward parts" in the Hebrew refers to the hidden womb of the heart.

God places His nature only in a heart that is:

- clean

- surrendered

- humble

- broken

- trembling

- purified

The fear of the Lord creates this inner womb—

a place where God can safely deposit:

- His Word

- His will

- His mind

- His truth

- His nature

- His assignments

- His anointing

2. FEAR IS THE ATMOSPHERE FOR DIVINE SEED TO BE PLANTED

1 John 3:9

"His seed remains in him…"

This "seed" (sperma) is:

- the Word

- the revelation

- the prophetic assignment

- the divine nature

- the spiritual DNA of God

This seed cannot be planted in:

- arrogant hearts

- distracted hearts

- double-minded hearts

- religious hearts

- proud hearts

- unclean hearts

86

Fear prepares the soil.

Fear breaks the ground.

Fear fertilizes the spirit.

Fear creates spiritual sensitivity.

This is why the fear of the Lord is clean—

because God only plants in clean soil.

3. DIVINE INTIMACY ALWAYS LEADS TO DIVINE CONCEPTION

Luke 1:35

> *"The Holy Spirit will come upon you,*
> *and the power of the Highest will overshadow you…"*

Mary's womb conceived because:

- her heart was humble

- her spirit feared God

- her life was pure

- her posture was surrender

What happened in the natural with Mary

happens in the spiritual with every believer:

- The Holy Spirit overshadows

- The Word enters

- The spirit conceives

- A calling forms

- Destiny grows

- Glory develops

- Purpose is birthed

But this only happens in a life that fears the Lord.

Fear opens the womb of the spirit.

4. FEAR OF THE LORD GUARDS THE WOMB OF PURPOSE

When a woman is pregnant, she protects the womb.

She becomes careful.

She avoids dangerous things.

Likewise, when God plants something in your spirit:

- the fear of the Lord protects it

- fear keeps you away from sin

- fear shields you from compromise

- fear separates you from the wrong people

- fear closes spiritual doors the enemy used to enter

- fear preserves your purity

- fear keeps your heart clean

The spiritual womb must be guarded.

The fear of the Lord is divine prenatal care—

preserving what God is forming in you.

5. FEAR OF THE LORD CAUSES THE WORD TO GERMINATE INSIDE YOU

James 1:21

"...receive with meekness the implanted word..."

Fear results in meekness.

Meekness produces receptivity.

Receptivity produces implantation.

Implantation produces germination.

Without fear:

- the Word stays on the surface

- truth bounces off

- conviction is resisted

- revelation is lost

- transformation never starts

But with fear:

- the Word enters

- the Word breaks

- the Word roots

- the Word grows

- the Word transforms

This is divine conception in action.

6. FEAR OF THE LORD MAKES YOU A CARRIER OF GOD'S NATURE

2 Peter 1:4

"...partakers of the divine nature..."

To partake means:

- to receive

- to absorb

- to carry

- to embody

Fear makes your heart safe for God's character to grow.

Satan cannot enter a heart filled with fear of the Lord.

Pride cannot survive in a heart filled with fear of the Lord.

Lust cannot thrive where the fear of the Lord dwells.

Fear becomes the environment where God's nature develops.

7. FEAR MAKES YOU IMPREGNATED WITH PURPOSE AND DESTINY

Every calling begins with fear.

Abraham's destiny began when he feared God (Gen. 22:12).

Moses' calling grew out of fear (Exod. 3:6).

David's kingship matured through fear (Ps. 34:11).

Mary's assignment was conceived through fear (Luke 1:50).

Jesus Himself delighted in fear (Isa. 11:2–3).

Fear is the divine incubator of destiny.

Without fear, destiny is miscarried.

8. FEAR BIRTHS SPIRITUAL FRUIT AND SUPERNATURAL AUTHORITY

Every pregnancy leads to birth.

When the fear of the Lord has produced:

- revelation

- holiness

- obedience

- purity

- maturity

- intimacy

…then the time comes for spiritual birthing.

This birthing produces:

- spiritual authority

- prophetic clarity

- apostolic courage

- intercessory power

- Holy Spirit fire

- discernment

- boldness

- revival impact

God births His nature in those who fear Him.

9. FEAR OF THE LORD LEADS TO UNION — UNION LEADS TO CONCEPTION — CONCEPTION LEADS TO BIRTHING

This is the divine pattern:

FEAR → UNION → CONCEPTION → DEVELOPMENT → BIRTHING → GLORY

Fear produces union.

Union produces conception.

Conception produces development.

Development produces birthing.

Birthing produces transformation.

Transformation produces God's glory in your life.

The fear of the Lord is not elementary—

it is the engine of spiritual reproduction.

10. A LIFE OF FEAR BECOMES A LIFE FULL OF GOD

When the fear of the Lord has matured in a believer,

their life becomes:

- a temple

- a womb

- a sanctuary

- a place of divine habitation

God does not just visit them—

He lives in them.

This is the highest form of intimacy.

This is union.

This is spiritual intercourse.

This is the formation of Christ inside the believer.

Galatians 4:19

"...until Christ is formed in you."

Christ is formed in those who fear Him.

CLOSING PRAYER (End of Chapter Nine)

Holy Father,

prepare the womb of my spirit

to receive Your seed,

Your Word,

Your nature,

Your calling,

and Your presence.

Let the fear of the Lord purify me,

break me,

cleanse me,

and empty me

until I am a holy vessel suitable for Your indwelling.

Conceive Your will within me.

Develop Your character in me.

Birth Your glory through me.

Make me one with You in purpose and purity

until Christ is fully formed in me.

In Jesus' holy name, Amen.

CHAPTER TEN:
THE FEAR OF THE LORD AND THE REALM OF DIVINE POSSESSION

How Holy Fear Leads to God Fully Occupying, Transforming, and Living Through the Believer

Psalm 19:9 — "The fear of the Lord is clean, enduring forever…"

Most Christians stop at salvation.

Some go further into the gifts.

A few enter intimacy.

Very few reach union.

But almost none enter this realm:

The realm of divine possession — where God fully occupies the inner man and expresses His life through the believer.

This is the realm of:

- Enoch

- Moses

- David

- Elijah

- Paul

- John

- Jesus

And every single person God fully inhabited had one foundational trait:

they feared the Lord above everything else.

Let's go deeper.

1. FEAR OF THE LORD EMPTIES THE VESSEL FOR GOD TO FILL

2 Timothy 2:21

"If a man therefore purges himself... he shall be a vessel unto honor..."

Fear purges a believer.

Fear cleans the vessel.

Fear removes:

- pride

- lust

- jealousy

- ambition

- selfish motives

- fleshly desires

- hidden sins

- secret attitudes

Fear empties a person until nothing remains but God.

A vessel must be empty before it can be filled.

Fear is the divine emptying process.

2. FEAR CREATES AN INNER STILLNESS THAT GOD CAN INHABIT

Psalm 46:10

"Be still and know that I am God."

Fear produces stillness.

Stillness produces knowing.

Knowing produces union.

The fear of the Lord quiets:

- emotional noise

- mental clutter

- fleshly impulses

- worldly distractions

- internal chaos

When the soul is still, God speaks.

When the soul is silent, God fills.

When the soul is surrendered, God dwells.

Fear creates the internal atmosphere where God can rest.

3. FEAR OF THE LORD OPENS THE INNER SANCTUARY TO GOD'S GLORY

The tabernacle had:

- outer court (salvation)

- inner court (service)

- holy place (ministry)

- holy of holies (presence, glory, revelation)

Fear is the key to the innermost chamber.

No fear = no holy of holies.

This is why Hebrews 12:28 says:

> *"...serve God acceptably with reverence and godly fear."*

Because only reverence invites glory.

Fear opens the inner sanctuary.

Glory fills it.

4. FEAR OF THE LORD ALLOWS GOD TO LIVE THROUGH THE BELIEVER

Galatians 2:20

"It is no longer I who live, but Christ lives in me…"

This is not poetry.

This is literal spiritual reality.

When fear matures in a believer:

- God thinks through them

- God speaks through them

- God prays through them

- God loves through them

- God heals through them

- God wars through them

- God reveals through them

- God leads through them

- God shines through them

Fear removes self so God can manifest Himself.

Fear does not make you disappear.

It makes God visible through you.

5. FEAR OF THE LORD PRODUCES A TRANSPARENT SOUL GOD CAN SHINE THROUGH

Matthew 5:8

"Blessed are the pure in heart, for they shall see God."

"Pure" means transparent — nothing hidden.

Fear:

- exposes

- humbles

- cleans

- refines

- purifies

- melts the soul

Fear removes opacity.

Fear removes darkness.

Fear removes fleshly filters.

The more transparent the soul,

the more clearly God can shine through it.

This is divine transfiguration.

6. FEAR OF THE LORD MAKES THE BELIEVER A "THRONE ROOM EXTENSION" ON EARTH

Psalm 25:14

"The secret of the Lord is with those who fear Him…"

Why?

Because those who fear Him are safe.

God cannot:

- speak deeply

- reveal greatly

- entrust heavily

- pour richly

- burden deeply

- use powerfully

…someone who lacks fear.

But when holy fear saturates a life, that believer becomes:

- a throne room representative

- a vessel of divine counsel

- a carrier of divine secrets

- a mouthpiece of heaven

- an ambassador of holiness

The fear of God makes you a portable holy of holies.

7. FEAR OF THE LORD BRINGS A MAN UNDER THE SPIRIT'S FULL AUTHORITY

Acts 5 reveals something shocking.

Before Ananias and Sapphira died,

the church had authority.

After they died,

the church had fear —

and then came unrestricted power.

Fear → authority.

Fear → purity.

Fear → supernatural boldness.

Fear → apostolic power.

Fear positions the believer under the Spirit's full command.

8. FEAR OF THE LORD IS THE FOUNDATION OF MYSTICAL UNION

Ephesians 3:19

"...that you may be filled with all the fullness of God..."

How?

Through fear.

Because fear:

- empties the vessel

- purifies the soul

- removes hindrances

- produces stillness

- births surrender

- attracts glory

- reveals God

- expands the spirit

- aligns the will

- opens the sanctuary

Fear prepares you for fullness.

Fullness means:

- the mind of Christ

- the heart of the Father

- the fire of the Spirit

- the nature of God

- the authority of Jesus

- the holiness of heaven

- the desires of God

Fear is what makes fullness possible.

9. FEAR OF THE LORD LEADS TO A LIFE WHERE GOD "TAKES OVER"

This is the deepest truth.

There is a point where fear has matured in a believer

so deeply and thoroughly

that God begins to take over the inner life:

- your thoughts become His thoughts

- your desires become His desires

- your words become His words

- your steps become His will

- your prayers become His burdens

- your vision becomes His eyes

- your heart becomes His heart

- your purpose becomes His purpose

This is divine possession —

holy, clean, pure, and glorious.

Fear prepares the vessel.

God fills it.

10. FEAR OF THE LORD IS THE PATHWAY TO THE FULLNESS OF CHRIST

Colossians 1:27

"...Christ in you, the hope of glory."

Not around you.

Not with you.

Not near you.

In you.

Fear is what creates a heart that Christ can fully inhabit.

Fear is the soil where glory takes root.

Fear is the doorway to fullness.

Fear is the environment of divine indwelling.

Fear is the atmosphere of transfiguration.

Fear is the womb of spiritual formation.

Fear is the secret chamber of divine union.

Fear is the foundation of life in God.

CLOSING PRAYER

Holy Father,

take me beyond intimacy,

beyond union,

beyond conception,

beyond revelation

into the realm of divine indwelling.

Empty me of everything that is not You

and fill me with everything that is You.

Possess my mind, my heart, my soul, and my spirit.

Let my life be an extension of Your throne room,

a vessel of Your presence,

a mirror of Your character,

and a carrier of Your glory.

Make me transparent

so that Christ may shine through me

with unhindered clarity.

In Jesus' holy name, Amen.

CHAPTER ELEVEN:
THE FEAR OF THE LORD AND THE REALM OF DIVINE REVELATION & VISITATION

How Holy Fear Opens the Heavens, Invites God's Voice, and Unlocks Last-Days Encounters

Blueprint of the Remnant, Part I

Psalm 19:9 — "The fear of the Lord is clean, enduring forever..."

Every remnant generation in Scripture was marked by:

- visions

- dreams

- angelic visitations

- prophetic encounters

- divine instructions

- heavenly revelations

From Noah to Moses,

from Daniel to John the Revelator—

they all walked in the fear of the Lord.

Fear is the key that unlocks heaven's realm.

This chapter will reveal the depth of how holy fear brings:

- divine visitations

- audible encounters

- prophetic dreams

- angelic assignment

- heavenly revelation

- throne room wisdom

- last-days instructions

Let's go deeper.

1. THE FEAR OF THE LORD OPENS THE EYES OF THE SPIRIT

Psalm 25:14

"The secret of the Lord is with those who fear Him..."

THIS IS NOT FIGURATIVE.

It means:

- revelation knowledge

- prophetic insight

- hidden mysteries

- divine warnings

- spiritual discernment

- open heaven access

- direct communication from God

Fear is the lens that clears the spiritual eyes.

Without fear, the inner eyes stay:

- dim

- clouded

- confused

- deceived

- distracted

The remnant sees because they fear.

2. FEAR ATTRACTS ANGELIC VISITATION

Psalm 34:7

"The angel of the Lord encamps around those who fear Him..."

Angels are drawn to fear.

Throughout Scripture:

- angels appeared to those who feared God (Daniel, Mary, Cornelius)

- angels delivered those who feared God

- angels strengthened those who feared God

- angels warned those who feared God

- angels carried messages to those who feared God

Where there is fear, there is heavenly activity.

The remnant Church will walk with angelic help because they walk in fear.

3. FEAR IS THE GATEWAY TO PROPHETIC ENCOUNTERS

Proverbs 1:23

> *"I will pour out My Spirit on you,*
> *I will make My words known to you."*

God reveals His voice to the reverent.

Religion hears sermons.

The remnant hears God.

Because the remnant fears Him.

Moses heard God from the burning bush.

Samuel heard God call him by name.

David heard God in the secret place.

Daniel heard God in visions.

Paul heard Jesus on the road to Damascus.

John heard the voice "like a trumpet."

All of them feared the Lord.

All of them were visited by God.

4. FEAR OF THE LORD CREATES A DWELLING PLACE FOR THE HOLY SPIRIT

Acts 5 reveals the severity of God's holiness—

but the chapter ends with:

> *"...and great power was upon them all."*

Why?

Because fear had been restored to the Church.

Fear cleans the vessel.

Fear opens the sanctuary.

Fear invites the Spirit to dwell without resistance.

A Church without fear has gifts.

A Church with fear has glory.

The remnant will walk in the fullness of the Spirit because they walk in holy fear.

5. FEAR PURIFIES THE SOUL SO GOD CAN SPEAK CLEARLY

Psalm 19:9

> *"The fear of the Lord is clean..."*

Fear cleans:

- motives

- attitudes

- thoughts

- desires

- emotions

- imagination

A clean soul receives a clean signal.

When the vessel is clean:

- no static

- no interference

- no confusion

- no mixture

- no distortion

The remnant hears God with clarity because their hearts are clean.

6. FEAR OF THE LORD POSITIONS THE REMNANT FOR LAST-DAYS REVELATION

Daniel 10 is one of the holiest chapters in Scripture.

Daniel saw powerful visions of the end times,

but the angel told him WHY:

"From the first day you set your heart to understand and to humble yourself..."

Humility = fear.

Daniel RECEIVED end-time revelation because he LIVED in fear.

Likewise, the remnant in the last days will receive prophetic intelligence from heaven:

- divine warnings

- prophetic timelines

- instructions for survival

- insights into world systems

- revelation of Babylon's fall

- clarity about the Beast system

- understanding of judgments

- preparation for Christ's return

Fear positions the remnant to see what others cannot.

7. FEAR OF THE LORD MAKES THE REMNANT A PORTAL OF HEAVEN

Wherever the fear of God rests, heaven opens.

Jacob saw the ladder.

Moses saw the cloud.

Joshua saw the Commander of the Lord's army.

Isaiah saw the throne.

Ezekiel saw the wheels and the glory.

Daniel saw the Ancient of Days.

Stephen saw Jesus standing.

John saw heaven opened.

All these men had one thing in common:

Deep, trembling fear of the Lord.

Fear builds the altar.

God builds the portal.

8. FEAR AWAKENS THE DISCERNMENT TO TEST VISITATIONS

Not every vision is from God.

Not every dream is spiritual.

Not every angelic appearance is holy.

2 Corinthians 11:14 warns:

"Satan himself transforms into an angel of light."

The ONLY protection from deception is the fear of the Lord.

Fear gives the remnant:

- spiritual detection

- discernment of spirits

- recognition of false light

- sensitivity to demonic presence

- clarity in testing revelations

Fear keeps the remnant from deception in the last days.

9. FEAR PREPARES THE REMNANT FOR THE COMING GLORY OUTPOURING

Haggai 2 prophesies:

"The glory of the latter house shall be greater…"

But who receives this glory?

Those who fear.

Psalm 85:9

> *"Surely His salvation is near to those who fear Him,*
> *that glory may dwell in our land."*

Fear precedes glory.

Glory rests on:

- clean hands

- pure hearts

- trembling spirits

- consecrated lives

Fear is the foundation for the last great outpouring.

10. FEAR OF THE LORD MAKES A BELIEVER TRUSTWORTHY FOR DIVINE SECRETS

Proverbs 25:2

> *"It is the glory of God to conceal a matter;*
> *it is the glory of kings to search it out."*

Who are the kings?

Those who fear Him.

Revelation 1:6

> *"He has made us kings and priests…"*

The remnant is a royal priesthood,

governed by:

- holiness

- consecration

- fear

- purity

God entrusts His deepest secrets only to those who fear Him.

The remnant will walk in such revelation that:

- the world will marvel

- religious people will reject them

- hell will fear them

- heaven will support them

Because they walk in the fear of the Lord.

CLOSING PRAYER

Holy Father,

open heaven over my life

and make me a vessel of divine revelation.

Purify my heart,

cleanse my motives,

sanctify my thoughts,

and remove every hindrance

that prevents me from hearing Your voice.

Let holy fear draw me into visions,

dreams,

instructions,

and throne-room encounters.

Make me part of Your last-days remnant

who walk in revelation,

discernment,

and divine visitation.

In Jesus' mighty name, Amen.

**CHAPTER TWELVE:
THE FEAR OF THE LORD:
HOW GOD TURNS THE
REMNANT INTO A LIVING
ARK OF THE COVENANT**

Blueprint of the Remnant, Part II

Psalm 19:9 — "The fear of the Lord is clean, enduring forever…"

In the Old Testament, the Ark of the Covenant was:

- the holiest object on earth

- the throne of God's presence

- the container of His glory

- the symbol of His covenant

- the resting place of His voice

- the center of Israel's identity

Only those who feared the Lord could stand near it.

Only the consecrated could carry it.

Only the clean could approach it.

Only the reverent survived it.

The Ark was not just a box.

It was the physical manifestation of God's presence.

In the New Testament, something astonishing happens:

God's presence no longer rests inside a golden chest.

It rests inside the believer.

2 Corinthians 6:16

> *"You are the temple of the living God."*

But not every believer carries the presence in fullness.

Only those whose lives resemble the Ark—

those who walk in the fear of the Lord.

Let's go deeper.

1. THE FEAR OF THE LORD MAKES THE REMNANT A RESTING PLACE FOR GOD'S GLORY

Psalm 132:14

> *"This is My resting place forever…"*

God does not rest on talent.

God does not rest on gifting.

God does not rest on emotion.

God does not rest on charisma.

God rests on holy fear.

Where there is fear:

- God rests

- God abides

- God dwells

- God reveals

- God manifests

Fear builds the throne.

God occupies it.

The remnant becomes a mobile Ark—

a walking resting place of God's glory.

2. THE ARK WAS COVERED IN GOLD — FEAR MAKES YOUR HEART PURE LIKE GOLD

Exodus 25:11

"Overlay it with pure gold..."

Gold in Scripture symbolizes:

- purity

- holiness

- divine nature

- tested faith

- glory

- refinement

Malachi 3:3 says God purifies believers like gold.

How?

Through the fear of the Lord.

Psalm 19:9 describes fear as clean—

fear purifies the heart until it becomes a vessel worthy of glory.

The remnant becomes a living Ark because fear turns the heart into gold.

3. THE ARK WAS A HOLY CONTAINER — FEAR MAKES YOU A CONTAINER OF GOD HIMSELF

The Ark of the Covenant contained:

1. The tablets of the Word

2. The manna

3. Aaron's rod that budded

Each object symbolizes what the remnant will carry.

A. The Word (The Tablets)

Fear of the Lord makes you a carrier of the Word—

not just in knowledge, but in nature.

- You live it

- You embody it

- You speak from it

- You tremble at it

Isaiah 66:2

> *"...the one who trembles at My Word."*

B. The Manna (The Presence)

Manna symbolizes:

- revelation

- daily presence

- supernatural provision

Fear leads to intimacy, which leads to daily manna—

fresh encounters with God.

C. Aaron's Rod (Authority)

The rod represents:

- resurrection life

- spiritual authority

- divine approval

Fear makes you trustworthy with authority.

Without fear, authority becomes corruption.

The remnant who fear God carry:

- His Word

- His presence

- His authority

Exactly like the Ark.

4. THE FEAR OF THE LORD PUTS THE REMNANT UNDER THE SHADOW OF THE MERCY SEAT

The Ark's lid was called the Mercy Seat—

the place where God's presence sat,

and mercy flowed.

The Mercy Seat symbolizes:

- covering

- forgiveness

- intercession

- compassion

- blood atonement

The remnant lives under the mercy seat

because fear produces:

- humility

- repentance

- dependence

- surrender

Fear makes the believer a vessel of mercy—

carrying Christ's compassion everywhere.

5. THE FEAR OF THE LORD MAKES YOU CARRY GOD'S VOICE LIKE THE ARK DID

Exodus 25:22

"There I will meet with you…
and I will speak with you…"

God spoke from the Ark.

Now He speaks from within the believer

—IF that believer fears Him.

Without fear:

- the voice is clouded

- the signal is distorted

- the spirit is dull

- the conscience is weak

But with fear:

- God's whisper becomes clear

- His instructions become sharp

- His guidance becomes constant

- His warnings become strong

- His presence becomes weighty

Fear gives the remnant a prophetic voice like the Ark.

6. THE FEAR OF THE LORD MAKES YOU UNTOUCHABLE BY THE WORLD

In 1 Samuel 5, when the Philistines touched the Ark,

judgment struck their entire camp.

Why?

The Ark was:

- holy

- consecrated

- untouchable by the unclean

Likewise, the remnant who fear God become untouchable:

- demonic attacks fail

- curses break

- witchcraft cannot land

- evil assignments collapse

- satanic plans reverse

The fear of the Lord builds a holy firewall around the remnant.

7. THE FEAR OF THE LORD MAKES YOU A CARRIER OF GOD'S POWER

When the Ark moved,

miracles moved:

- Jordan River parted

- Jericho walls fell

- enemies were destroyed

- plagues broke out

- victories erupted

Why?

Because God was with the Ark.

When the remnant walks in fear:

- spiritual authority increases

- prophetic power rises

- miracles manifest

- boldness comes

- heaven moves with them

Fear turns the remnant into walking portals of divine power.

8. THE FEAR OF THE LORD MAKES YOU A HOLY TERROR TO THE ENEMY

1 Samuel 5:7

"Send away the Ark... for His hand is harsh against us."

The enemy fears the vessels God inhabits.

The remnant who carry God's presence become:

- spiritually dangerous

- divinely protected

- untouchable

- a threat to darkness

- destroyers of demonic camps

Fear of the Lord produces fearlessness of the enemy.

When you fear God, the enemy fears you.

9. THE FEAR OF THE LORD KEEPS YOU FROM PROFANING GOD'S PRESENCE

Uzzah died because he touched the Ark without reverence.

The message is clear:

God's presence is not casual.

Remnant carriers must:

- walk humbly

- guard purity

- honor God's presence

- never trivialize the holy

- live in constant reverence

Fear keeps the remnant from defiling the glory they carry.

10. THE REMNANT BECOMES A WALKING ARK — A MOBILE THRONE OF GOD

Revelation 21:3

"Behold, the dwelling place of God is with men..."

This prophecy begins NOW—

in the remnant.

Fear turns a believer into:

- a dwelling place

- a holy container

- a carrier of the covenant

- a keeper of the presence

- a resting place for glory

- a throne of God in motion

- a walking holy of holies

This is the end-time remnant:

Living Arks of the Covenant.

Mobile mercy seats.

Walking sanctuaries.

Carriers of glory.

Hosts of the presence.

Guardians of the fire.

CLOSING PRAYER

Holy Father,

make me a living Ark of the Covenant.

Overlay my heart with Your purity.

Fill me with Your Word,

Your presence,

and Your authority.

Cover me under Your mercy seat

and speak through me as You did from the Ark of old.

Let Your fear guard my life

so Your glory can rest on me without hindrance.

Make me a carrier of Your presence,

a vessel of honor,

and a holy dwelling place for Your fire.

In Jesus' mighty name, Amen.

CHAPTER THIRTEEN: THE FEAR OF THE LORD PREPARES THE BRIDE FOR THE RETURN OF THE KING

Blueprint of the Remnant, Part III

Psalm 19:9 — "The fear of the Lord is clean, enduring forever…"

The return of Jesus Christ is the greatest event in the history of the universe.

It is the moment when:

- the Bridegroom returns for His Bride

- the dead in Christ rise

- the living remnant are transformed

- the kingdoms of this world collapse

- judgment falls on the wicked

- heaven and earth converge

- the King takes His throne

But Scripture is clear:

Only a certain type of believer will be ready.

Not the religious.

Not the casual.

Not the lukewarm.

Not the worldly.

Not the crowd-Christian.

Only the remnant—those who walk in the fear of the Lord—will be prepared as the Bride of Christ.

The fear of the Lord is not just holiness.

It is bridal preparation.

It is spiritual beautification.

It is divine refinement.

It is the oil in the lamp.

Let's go deeper.

1. THE FEAR OF THE LORD IS THE OIL OF THE BRIDE

Matthew 25:4

The foolish virgins had lamps (salvation),

but no oil (fear, intimacy, obedience).

They were not ready.

They were shut out.

The wise virgins carried oil—

oil produced by:

- holy fear

- reverence

- purity

- obedience

- surrender

- devotion

- watchfulness

The fear of the Lord is the oil that keeps the flame burning.

Without fear, the lamp goes out.

2. THE FEAR OF THE LORD IS THE GARMENT OF THE BRIDE

Revelation 19:7–8

"…His wife has made herself ready.
To her it was granted to be arrayed in fine linen, clean and bright,
for the fine linen is the righteous acts of the saints."

The Bride's garments are righteous acts

—clean, pure, holy living.

Fear produces righteousness.

Fear produces obedience.

Fear produces purity.

Fear produces a lifestyle worthy of the wedding.

The Bride cannot wear a garment of sin and expect the King to approve.

Fear clothes the Bride in holiness.

3. THE FEAR OF THE LORD MAKES THE BRIDE WATCHFUL AND AWAKE

Luke 12:37

"Blessed are those servants whom the Master finds watching…"

Fear creates:

- alertness

- spiritual sensitivity

- awareness of the times

- discernment

- readiness

- sobriety

A Bride who fears the Lord is never distracted.

Never sleeping.

Never spiritually dull.

Fear keeps her awake.

Fear keeps her burning.

Fear keeps her ready.

4. THE FEAR OF THE LORD PURIFIES THE BRIDE FOR THE GRAND APPEARING

1 John 3:2–3

> *"When He appears, we shall be like Him…*
> *everyone who has this hope purifies himself."*

Purification is not optional.

It is mandatory for the Bride.

Fear:

- cleanses

- refines

- sanctifies

- washes

- transforms

- perfects the inner man

Fear is the internal spiritual bath

that prepares the Bride for the appearing of her King.

5. THE FEAR OF THE LORD MAKES THE BRIDE DESIRE THE BRIDEGROOM ABOVE ALL ELSE

Religion desires blessings.

The Bride desires the Bridegroom.

Religion desires positions.

The Bride desires nearness.

Religion desires gifts.

The Bride desires His face.

Religion desires comfort.

The Bride desires holiness.

Fear shifts the heart from:

- selfishness to devotion

- gifts to Giver

- blessings to presence

- religion to relationship

Fear produces love.

Fear produces longing.

Fear produces desire for Jesus Himself.

This is bridal love.

6. THE FEAR OF THE LORD SEPARATES THE BRIDE FROM THE WORLD

James 4:4

> *"...friendship with the world is enmity with God."*

Fear breaks:

- worldly habits

- worldly desires

- worldly attachments

- worldly influences

- worldly mindset

Fear sanctifies.

Fear consecrates.

Fear sets apart.

The Bride cannot be worldly.

The Bride must be separate.

The Bride must resemble heaven—not earth.

Fear makes the Bride holy.

7. THE FEAR OF THE LORD GIVES THE BRIDE EARS TO HEAR THE BRIDEGROOM'S VOICE

Revelation 2:7

"He who has an ear, let him hear…"

Many in the last days will be deaf:

- deaf to conviction

- deaf to truth

- deaf to warnings

- deaf to the Spirit

- deaf to prophecy

* deaf to the Bridegroom's call

But the remnant Bride hears Him because she fears Him.

Fear opens the spiritual ear.

Fear sharpens discernment.

Fear tunes the heart to His whisper.

8. THE FEAR OF THE LORD GUARDS THE BRIDE FROM DECEPTION

Matthew 24:24

"...false Christs and false prophets will rise..."

The last days will be full of:

* lying signs

* false wonders

* counterfeit anointings

* deceptive doctrines

* seducing spirits

The only safeguard is the fear of the Lord.

Fear:

* exposes falsehood

* unmasks deception

* protects purity

* shields the heart

* illuminates truth

Fear keeps the Bride from being seduced by imposters.

9. THE FEAR OF THE LORD GIVES THE BRIDE HOLY BOLDNESS FOR THE FINAL HOUR

Esther feared the King,

not the throne.

Daniel feared God,

not lions.

Shadrach, Meshach, and Abednego feared the Lord,

not fire.

The apostles feared God,

not persecution.

Fear of the Lord removes fear of everything else.

The Bride will need holy boldness in the final hour:

- to endure persecution

- to resist compromise

- to reject the Beast system

- to stand in holiness

- to proclaim Jesus fearlessly

Fear produces courage.

10. THE FEAR OF THE LORD MAKES THE BRIDE LONG FOR THE RETURN OF JESUS

Revelation 22:17

The Bride calls for Him.

Not because she is desperate.

But because she loves Him.

Fear of the Lord produces:

- awe

- longing

- anticipation

- yearning

- love

- devotion

A Bride who fears the Lord is not afraid of His return—

she longs for it.

She lives for it.

She prepares for it.

She cries out for it.

CLOSING PRAYER

Holy Father,

prepare my heart as the Bride

for the coming of the King.

Clothe me in holiness,

fill my vessel with oil,

wash my garments in purity,

and keep my lamp burning.

Let the fear of the Lord

purify me,

separate me,

sanctify me,

and make me watchful.

Give me eyes to see,

ears to hear,

and a heart that longs only for Jesus.

Make me ready for the wedding supper of the Lamb.

Come, Lord Jesus. Amen.

CHAPTER FOURTEEN: THE FEAR OF THE LORD INVITES THE FIRE, GLORY, AND JUDGMENTS OF GOD

Blueprint of the Remnant, Part IV

Psalm 19:9 — "The fear of the Lord is clean, enduring forever…"

In Scripture, whenever the fear of the Lord appears, three forces always follow:

1. The Fire of God – cleansing, consuming, empowering

2. The Glory of God – weight, presence, revelation

3. The Judgments of God – divine order, justice, holiness

The remnant is the generation that will experience ALL THREE at once.

The last-days Church will not survive without holy fear, because fear is the ONLY atmosphere where:

- fire falls safely

- glory rests permanently

- judgment purifies without destroying

This chapter will show how the remnant—governed by the fear of the Lord—becomes the chosen vessel through which God releases His fire, carries His glory, and executes His judgments on the earth.

Let's go deeper.

1. THE FEAR OF THE LORD IS THE ENVIRONMENT WHERE GOD'S FIRE FALLS

Leviticus 9:23–24

> *"The glory of the Lord appeared... then fire came out from before the Lord..."*

Fire and glory are inseparable.

Fire always follows glory.

Glory always follows fear.

Fear → Glory

Glory → Fire

Where there is no fear of God,

He will not send His fire.

Because:

- fire purifies

- fire exposes

- fire consumes flesh

- fire destroys idols

- fire burns sin

- fire ignites holiness

Only the remnant, purified by fear, can carry God's fire without being consumed.

2. FEAR OF THE LORD CLEANSES THE ALTAR SO FIRE CAN FALL

1 Kings 18

Elijah repaired the altar FIRST—

THEN fire fell.

The altar symbolizes:

- the heart

- the soul

- the motives

- the inner life

- the posture of worship

Fear of the Lord repairs the altar.

Without fear:

- the altar is broken

- the heart is divided

- worship is shallow

- motives are impure

Fire cannot fall on a broken altar.

Fear rebuilds the altar.

Fire ignites it.

3. THE FEAR OF THE LORD INVITES GOD'S VISIBLE GLORY

2 Chronicles 5:14

> *"The priests could not stand... for the glory of the Lord filled the house of God."*

They could not stand because GOD was standing.

But why did the glory come?

Because the priests were:

- consecrated

- Trembling

- Reverent

- obedient

- pure

Fear produces an atmosphere where God feels welcome.

Fear dethrones flesh so God's throne can descend.

A remnant walking in fear becomes a living glory chamber.

4. FEAR OF THE LORD MAKES THE BELIEVER A CARRIER OF GOD'S WEIGHT

The Hebrew word for "glory" is kabod—

meaning weight, heaviness, substance.

The weight of God cannot rest on:

- carnal hearts

- proud leaders

- religious systems

- impure vessels

Only the remnant can carry the weight of God because fear:

- stabilizes the soul

- strengthens character

- produces humility

- creates solidity

- anchors the heart

Fear makes you spiritually strong enough to carry glory.

5. FEAR OF THE LORD BRINGS HOLY FEAR AND JUDGMENT UPON THE ENEMY CAMP

Acts 5

Ananias and Sapphira fell dead because they lied in the atmosphere of glory.

But their death released something:

Holy fear upon the whole Church.

And after fear entered,

power multiplied.

Fear → Judgment

Judgment → Purity

Purity → Power

This pattern will return in the last days.

God's judgments will begin in the Church

to purify the remnant

before He judges the world.

6. FEAR OF THE LORD MAKES THE REMNANT A VESSEL OF DIVINE JUSTICE

Psalm 149:6–9 reveals a prophetic reality:

> *"Let the high praises of God be in their mouth,*
> *and a two-edged sword in their hand,*
> *to execute vengeance on the nations..."*

This is an end-time picture of the remnant.

They will:

- proclaim truth

- expose deception

- judge wickedness

- overthrow darkness

- pronounce divine justice

- partner with heaven's judgments

Fear prepares the remnant for this role.

Only a pure, trembling heart can carry divine justice safely.

7. THE FEAR OF THE LORD CAUSES THE REMNANT TO BECOME FIRE THEMSELVES

Jeremiah 20:9

> *"His word was in my heart like a burning fire..."*

When fear is full-grown in a believer:

- their prayer becomes fire

- their voice becomes fire

- their preaching becomes fire

- their worship becomes fire

- their presence becomes fire

Fear transforms you into a burning one.

Like John the Baptist:

> *"He was a burning and shining lamp."*
> *(John 5:35)*

Fear makes you burn.

Fire makes you shine.

8. THE FEAR OF THE LORD MAKES THE REMNANT A PLACE WHERE GOD JUDGES SIN

1 Peter 4:17

> *"Judgment must begin at the house of God."*

Judgment does not fall randomly.

It falls where fear has prepared the ground.

The remnant will experience:

- judgment on sin

- judgment on compromise

- judgment on hypocrisy

- judgment on deception

Not to destroy—

but to purify.

When the remnant is purified,

their purity becomes a standard

against which God judges the world.

9. THE FEAR OF THE LORD OPENS THE CLOUD OF GLORY LIKE IN THE DAYS OF MOSES

Exodus 33:18–22

Moses asked to see God's glory.

But first God placed him:

- in the cleft of the rock

- covered by His hand

- protected by His mercy

Why ?

Because glory demands holy fear.

Glory demands reverence.

Glory demands surrender.

The remnant will once again walk in:

- cloud glory

- presence glory

- transforming glory

- face-to-face glory

This is the inheritance of the fearful.

10. THE FEAR OF THE LORD IS THE FOUNDATION OF THE FINAL OUTPOURING OF FIRE AND GLORY

Joel 2 prophesies:

- visions

- dreams

- prophecy

- fire

- signs

- wonders

- end-time revival

But before the outpouring, God commands:

That is the fear of the Lord.

Fear comes before fire.

Fear comes before glory.

Fear comes before judgment.

The remnant will see:

- God's fire

- God's glory

- God's judgments

- God's power

- God's manifestation

- God's presence

Because they walk in holy fear.

CLOSING PRAYER

Holy Father,

baptize me in the fear of the Lord

so, I may carry Your fire,

Your glory,

and Your holy judgments.

Purify the altar of my heart,

let Your presence rest on me

and Your fire burn within me.

Make me a vessel of glory,

a carrier of Your weight,

and a partner in Your purposes.

Use me in these last days

to shine Your fire,

carry Your glory,

and uphold Your justice.

In Jesus' mighty name, Amen.

CHAPTER FIFTEEN:
THE FEAR OF THE LORD AND THE IDENTITY OF THE END-TIME REMNANT CHURCH

Blueprint of the Remnant, Part V

Psalm 19:9 — "The fear of the Lord is clean, enduring forever…"

In the last days, God will not use the entire visible Church.

He will not work through denominations, buildings, or religious systems.

He will work through a remnant—a purified, consecrated body that is marked by the fear of the Lord.

This remnant is:

- small

- hidden

- persecuted

- misunderstood

- rejected by religious people

- unknown to many

- but fully known by heaven

Their identity is not drawn from the world,

not from culture,

not from religion,

but from the fear of the Lord.

This chapter reveals the identity markers of the end-time remnant.

Let's go deeper.

1. THE REMNANT IS MARKED BY PURITY, NOT POPULARITY

Isaiah 1:9

"Unless the Lord of hosts had left to us a very small remnant…"

The remnant is small, not large.

They are not popular.

They are not platform-driven.

They are not crowd-focused.

They are purity-focused,

because the fear of the Lord demands holiness.

Their identity is not in numbers—

it is in consecration.

2. THE REMNANT FEARS GOD MORE THAN THEY FEAR MAN

Acts 5:29

"We must obey God rather than men."

The remnant:

- stands when others bow

- speaks when others stay silent

- obeys when others compromise

- follows God even unto death

Fear of the Lord builds immovable devotion.

Their identity is bold obedience

—not social approval.

3. THE REMNANT WALKS IN HUMILITY, NOT SELF-GLORY

Micah 6:8

"What does the Lord require of you… to walk humbly with your God?"

Humility is the remnant's signature.

Fear produces humility.

Humility attracts God's presence.

The remnant:

- carries no pride

- exalts no flesh

- seeks no platform

- glorifies no man

- boasts only in God

They are hidden, so God can be seen.

4. THE REMNANT IS SEPARATED FROM RELIGION AND WORLDLINESS

Revelation 18 :4

"Come out of her, My people…"

The remnant is separated from:

- false doctrine

- counterfeit Christianity

- worldly compromise

- lukewarm living

- Jezebel teaching

- Babylon systems

- dead religion

Their identity is holiness.

Their home is Zion, not Babylon.

They walk a narrow path because they fear the Lord.

5. THE REMNANT IS FILLED WITH THE WORD, NOT OPINION

Jeremiah 15:16

"Your words were found, and I ate them…"

The remnant devours the Word.

It is their food.

Their fire.

Their foundation.

They do not preach culture.

They do not preach trends.

They do not preach motivational fluff.

They preach:

- the Word

- the truth

- righteousness

- holiness

- repentance

- Christ crucified

The fear of the Lord makes the Word their identity.

6. THE REMNANT IS A PEOPLE OF PRAYER AND INTERCESSION

Joel 2:17

The remnant prays with:

- tears

- burden

- urgency

- travail

- groaning

- intercession

They don't offer religious prayers.

They offer spirit-born, fire-filled, heaven-moving prayer.

Fear births prayer.

Prayer births power.

7. THE REMNANT WALKS IN SUPERNATURAL DISCERNMENT

1 John 4:1

"Do not believe every spirit… test the spirits…"

The remnant cannot be deceived easily.

Their identity is sharpened discernment:

- they detect false teachers

- they discern lying spirits

- they recognize counterfeit anointing

- they see through deception

156

- they test the spirits

- they discern the times

Fear gives them spiritual eyes,

because fear makes the heart clean.

A clean heart sees clearly.

8. THE REMNANT IS HUNGRY FOR GOD, NOT FOR THE WORLD

Psalm 42:2

"My soul thirsts for God..."

The remnant is addicted to His presence.

They love holiness.

They chase purity.

They crave righteousness.

They seek His face more than blessing.

They desire intimacy above ministry.

Fear fuels hunger.

Hunger feeds intimacy.

Intimacy shapes identity.

9. THE REMNANT IS UNASHAMED OF THE GOSPEL

Romans 1:16

"I am not ashamed of the gospel of Christ..."

The remnant:

*   will preach truth boldly

*   confront sin courageously

*   expose deception fearlessly

*   stand against compromise

*   declare righteousness

*   call people to repentance

*   proclaim Jesus without fear

The fear of the Lord removes the fear of man.

10. THE REMNANT IS PREPARED TO SUFFER FOR CHRIST

Philippians 1:29

> *"To you it has been granted... to suffer for His sake."*

The remnant is unshaken by persecution.

They understand:

*   suffering purifies

*   suffering glorifies God

*   suffering produces endurance

*   suffering perfects faith

*   suffering prepares the Bride

Fear of the Lord empowers them to endure:

*   pain

- rejection

- slander

- accusations

- betrayal

- loneliness

- loss

- martyrdom

Their identity is loyalty in suffering.

11. THE REMNANT IS CLOTHED IN THE POWER OF THE HOLY SPIRIT

Acts 1:8

"You shall receive power after the Holy Spirit comes upon you…"

The remnant is not powerless.

They walk in:

- authority

- anointing

- discernment

- prophetic fire

- miracles

- deliverance

- revelation

- heaven's backing

Because the fear of the Lord creates a vessel worthy of power.

12. THE REMNANT IS THE TRUE CHURCH — THE BRIDE, THE OVERCOMERS, THE FAITHFUL

Revelation labels them:

- those who overcome

- those who keep their garments clean

- those who follow the Lamb wherever He goes

- those who are sealed

- those who escape deception

- those who endure

- those who remain loyal even unto death

This is their identity.

Fear forms them.

Fire refines them.

Glory fills them.

Judgment purifies them.

Holiness sustains them.

Presence empowers them.

They are the last-days remnant.

CLOSING PRAYER

Holy Father,

form me into a true remnant believer.

Shape my identity by Your fear,

purity,

holiness,

and truth.

Remove worldly desires,

break religious influence,

and separate me completely unto Yourself.

Give me hunger for Your presence,

boldness for Your truth,

discernment for the times,

and endurance for the coming days.

Mark me as Your remnant—

faithful, fearless, and fully Yours.

In Jesus' mighty name, Amen.

CHAPTER SIXTEEN:
THE FEAR OF THE LORD AND THE RISE OF THE END-TIME REMNANT ARMY

Blueprint of the Remnant, Part VI

Psalm 19:9 — "The fear of the Lord is clean, enduring forever…"

There is a final army rising in the earth—

not a military army,

not a political army,

not a religious army,

but a spiritual army formed, purified, and governed by the fear of the Lord.

This is the army the prophets saw.

The army Joel described.

The army Ezekiel foresaw.

The army Daniel hinted at.

The army John saw standing with the Lamb on Mount Zion.

This remnant army is:

- holy

- disciplined

- fearless

- pure

- uncompromising

- unstoppable

- unshakable

- filled with the Spirit

- governed by the fear of God

Let's go deeper into their rise.

1. THE REMNANT ARMY IS BORN FROM THE FEAR OF THE LORD

Isaiah 11:2–3 says of Jesus:

"The Spirit of the fear of the Lord... and His delight was in the fear of the Lord."

If even the Son of God walked in fear,

how much more His army?

Fear produces:

- discipline

- purity

- obedience

- submission

- holiness

The remnant army rises from the womb of holy fear.

Fear is their:

- training ground

- identity

- motivation

- strength

- atmosphere

2. THE FEAR OF THE LORD MAKES THE REMNANT ARMY IMMUNE TO FEAR OF MAN

Proverbs 29:25

"The fear of man brings a snare…"

The end-time army CANNOT fear:

- governments

- persecution

- threats

- prison

- death

- rejection

- hardship

- pressure

- the Antichrist system

Because they fear only the Lord.

Fear of God breaks fear of man.

Fear of God breaks fear of death.

Fear of God breaks fear of suffering.

This is why the remnant army cannot be stopped.

3. THE REMNANT ARMY IS TRAINED IN RIGHTEOUSNESS AND PURITY

Joel 2:11

"The Lord gives voice before His army..."

Why does He speak to THEM and not to everyone?

Because they are purified.

Joel 2 describes them as:

- running with precision

- climbing walls

- not breaking ranks

- not stumbling

- marching in unity

These are not carnal Christians.

They are refined warriors.

Fear produces:

- clean motives

- pure hearts

- holy habits

- disciplined lives

They fight sin before they fight demons.

4. THE REMNANT ARMY MOVES WITH SUPERNATURAL UNITY

Joel 2:7–8

> *"...each marches in his own column;*
> *they do not break ranks..."*

Unity is not natural.

Unity is supernatural.

Fear of the Lord produces unity because:

- pride dies

- ego dies

- competition dies

- jealousy dies

- self-will dies

The remnant army moves like ONE BODY because they fear the SAME LORD.

Where there is fear of God,

there is no room for rebellion.

5. THE REMNANT ARMY HEARS AND OBEYS THE COMMANDS OF THE KING

Psalm 110:3

*"Your people shall be volunteers
in the day of Your power…"*

They are "volunteers"—

willing, eager, surrendered.

They obey without delay:

- when He says "Go," they go

- when He says "Speak," they speak

- when He says "Stand," they stand

- when He says, "Be silent," they are silent

Fear produces instant obedience.

Disobedience is impossible for those who tremble before God.

6. THE REMNANT ARMY WALKS IN SUPERNATURAL POWER

Daniel 11:32

*"The people who know their God shall be strong and carry out great
exploits."*

"Know" here means intimacy rooted in fear.

Those who fear God:

- cast out demons

- heal the sick

- raise the dead

- prophesy accurately

- operate in miracles

- walk in boldness

- confront darkness

- command atmospheres

- shift nations

This army moves in power, not emotion.

In authority, not theatrics.

In revelation, not imagination.

7. THE REMNANT ARMY IS A PROPHETIC PEOPLE

Joel 2:28

"I will pour out My Spirit… your sons and daughters shall prophesy…"

Fear unlocks prophetic depth.

This army:

- hears God's voice

- sees visions

- dreams dreams

- receives divine strategies

- understands mysteries

- discerns spirits

- interprets times

They do not guess.

They do not assume.

They do not imitate.

They speak as God speaks.

8. THE REMNANT ARMY IS A WORSHIPING ARMY

Revelation 14 :1–3

"A Lamb standing on Mount Zion, and with Him 144,000..."

This army SINGS a new song.

Why ?

Because fear leads to intimacy.

Intimacy leads to worship.

Worship leads to revelation.

Revelation leads to warfare.

They fight through worship.

They war with praise.

They advance through adoration.

Fear keeps their worship pure.

9. THE REMNANT ARMY IS A SEPARATED ARMY

2 Timothy 2:4

"No soldier entangles himself with the affairs of this life…"

They are NOT distracted.

They do not:

- chase money

- chase status

- chase entertainment

- chase comfort

- chase popularity

They chase GOD.

Fear keeps them detached from the world

and attached to the King.

10. THE REMNANT ARMY IS THE ARMY THAT WILL STAND WITH JESUS AT HIS RETURN

Revelation 17 :14

"Those who are with Him are called, chosen, and faithful."

Three qualities:

- Called

- Chosen

- Faithful

This is the remnant army.

They are chosen because they fear God.

They are faithful because they fear God.

They will stand with the Lamb because they fear God.

This army overcomes:

- the beast

- the system

- the false prophet

- the persecution

- the deception

- the world

- the flesh

- the dragon

Fear of the Lord makes them unstoppable.

CLOSING PRAYER

Holy Father,

form me into a warrior of the end-time remnant army.

Train my hands for war,

my heart for purity,

my mind for Scripture,

and my spirit for obedience.

Clothe me with boldness,

fill me with fire,

strengthen me with holiness,

and govern me by the fear of the Lord.

Make me fearless before men

and faithful before You.

Count me among the called,

the chosen,

and the faithful—

an end-time warrior who stands with the Lamb.

In Jesus' mighty name, Amen.

CHAPTER SEVENTEEN: THE FEAR OF THE LORD AND THE REFINING OF THE END-TIME FIRE

Blueprint of the Remnant, Part VII

Psalm 19:9 — "The fear of the Lord is clean, enduring forever…"

Before God uses a vessel greatly,

He refines it deeply.

Before He displays a people publicly,

He purifies them privately.

Before He sends the remnant into the final conflict,

He takes them through the furnace of refinement.

This is not punishment.

This is preparation.

God is not trying to destroy the remnant—

He is trying to purify,

strengthen,

perfect,

and prepare them for glory.

And the catalyst of all refinement is the fear of the Lord.

Let's go deeper.

1. THE FEAR OF THE LORD LEADS YOU INTO THE FIRE

Malachi 3:2–3

*"For He is like a refiner's fire and like fullers' soap.
He will sit as a refiner… He will purify the sons of Levi…"*

The sons of Levi were the priests.

Today, YOU are a priest.

God refines His priests.

But what leads you into the fire?

The fear of the Lord.

Fear opens the door to refinement because fear says:

- "Lord, change me."

- "Lord, purify me."

- "Lord, correct me."

- "Lord, remove anything that offends You."

- "Lord, make me holy."

Fear invites purification.

2. GOD HIMSELF SITS AS THE REFINER OVER THE REMNANT

Malachi 3:3

"He will sit as a refiner."

A refiner NEVER leaves the fire.

He sits by the furnace and watches the gold.

He controls the temperature.

He monitors the process.

He oversees the transformation.

Likewise:

God never leaves you in the fire alone.

He watches every moment.

He increases heat only when necessary.

He lowers heat when you're overwhelmed.

Fear of the Lord ensures your refinement is divinely supervised.

3. THE FIRE REMOVES WHAT FLESH CANNOT REMOVE

Zechariah 13:9

"I will bring the third part through the fire...

The remnant is the "third part"—

the purified portion.

There are things in you that:

- fasting alone cannot remove

- prayer alone cannot remove

- teaching alone cannot remove

- discipline alone cannot remove

Only FIRE can remove:

- pride

- hidden sin

- fleshly ambition

- emotional wounds

- unforgiveness

- secret idols

- self-righteousness

- religious attitudes

- spiritual laziness

Fear brings you to the fire.

Fire removes the flesh.

4. THE REFINING FIRE EXPOSES WHAT IS UNSURRENDERED

Isaiah 48:10

*"Behold, I have refined you...
I have chosen you in the furnace of affliction."*

Refinement is not about punishment.

It's about exposure.

Fire reveals:

- motives

- hidden attitudes

- impure desires

- unconfessed sin

- broken areas

- resentments

- prideful tendencies

Fear says:

"Lord, reveal what must die."

Fire answers that prayer.

The remnant is refined because they invite God to expose the impure.

5. FIRE MAKES THE REMNANT SHINE LIKE GOD'S GOLD

Job 23:10

"When He has tested me, I shall come forth as gold."

Gold does not shine because it is gold.

It shines because it has been refined.

The remnant shines because:

- they endured the furnace

- they embraced humility

- they yielded to pruning

- they submitted to correction

- they allowed God to burn impurity

Fear leads to refinement.

Refinement leads to shine.

This shine is God's glory visible on a purified life.

6. FIRE PRODUCES SPIRITUAL AUTHORITY

Acts 2:3

> *"Tongues as of fire sat upon each of them."*

Before the disciples received:

- power

- authority

- boldness

- miracles

- gifts

- tongues

- signs

- wonders

They had to go through:

- fear

- surrender

- obedience

- waiting

- emptiness

- refinement

Fire came AFTER fear was restored in them.

The remnant army receives fire only because they carry pure fear.

7. FIRE REMOVES THE REMNANT FROM THE WORLD'S SYSTEM

1 Peter 1:7

> *"...the genuineness of your faith,*
> *being much more precious than gold that perishes,*
> *though it is tested by fire..."*

Fire is separation.

Fire divides.

Refinement removes:

- worldly desires

- carnal attachments

- emotional addictions

- people who hinder destiny

- relationships that corrupt holiness

- habits that weaken spirit

- desires that war against righteousness

Fire frees the remnant from the world.

Fear calls them to be different.

Fire makes them different.

8. THE REMNANT IS REFINED TO CARRY END-TIME GLORY

Psalm 24:3–4

> *"Who may ascend the hill of the Lord?*
> *He who has clean hands and a pure heart..."*

Clean hands = purified actions

Pure heart = refined motives

This is the remnant.

Fire prepares them for:

- the glory that is coming

- the outpouring of the Spirit

- the return of Jesus

- the great shaking

- the final harvest

- the judgments of God

- the final conflict with darkness

Without refinement, they cannot carry glory.

With refinement, they become glory vessels.

9. FIRE PREPARES THE REMNANT FOR END-TIME PERSECUTION

Daniel 11:35

"Some of the wise shall fall... to refine them, purify them, and make them white—until the time of the end..."

Persecution is not punishment.

It is refinement.

The remnant who survive the last hour are those who embraced refinement before persecution came.

Fear produces endurance.

Fire produces strength.

Together they make the remnant unbreakable.

10. FIRE MAKES THE REMNANT LOOK LIKE JESUS

Romans 8:29

"...to be conformed to the image of His Son."

Refinement is transformation.

The more fire you go through with fear,

the more you resemble Him:

- His purity

- His humility

- His holiness

- His character

- His love

- His righteousness

- His authority

- His endurance

- His fire

The remnant emerge from the furnace looking like Jesus Himself.

This is the purpose of refinement.

CLOSING PRAYER

Holy Father,

take me through the refining fire.

Remove every impurity,

every hidden sin,

every prideful thought,

every ungodly desire,

and every part of me that does not reflect Jesus.

Sit as the Refiner over my life.

Purify me like gold.

Strengthen me in the furnace.

Transform me into the image of Your Son.

Prepare me as a purified vessel

for the glory, fire, and calling of the last days.

In Jesus' mighty name, Amen.

CHAPTER EIGHTEEN: THE FEAR OF THE LORD AND THE SEPARATION OF THE REMNANT FROM BABYLON

Blueprint of the Remnant, Part VIII

Psalm 19:9 — "The fear of the Lord is clean, enduring forever…"

Before the return of Jesus,

before the rise of the Beast system,

before the Day of the Lord,

before the final shaking—

God issues one of the most urgent commands in all of Scripture:

Revelation 18 :4

HER = Babylon

The final world-religious-political-economic system.

A system of:

- seduction

- immorality

- idolatry

- deception

- greed

- witchcraft

- rebellion

- counterfeit religion

Babylon is not just a place.

It is a spirit.

A culture.

A mindset.

A system.

A kingdom of darkness.

Only one type of believer will escape her influence:

the remnant who walk in the fear of the Lord.

Let's go deeper.

1. THE FEAR OF THE LORD IS THE POWER THAT BREAKS BABYLON'S SPELL

Revelation 17 calls Babylon:

"The great harlot…
with whom the kings of the earth committed fornication."

This refers to:

- spiritual seduction

- compromised worship

- false unity

- corrupted religion

- counterfeit holiness

- pleasure-driven Christianity

- world-attraction

Babylon seduces Christians through:

- entertainment

- comfort

- pride

- greed

- sin tolerance

- false teaching

- emotional spirituality

- mixture with the world

- "self first" Christianity

The ONLY power strong enough to break Babylon's seduction

is the fear of the Lord.

Fear sobers.

Fear awakens.

Fear separates.

Fear protects.

Fear breaks deception.

2. THE FEAR OF THE LORD SEPARATES THE REMNANT FROM COMPROMISE

2 Corinthians 6:17

"Come out from among them
and be separate, says the Lord."

The remnant does not tolerate:

- partial obedience

- moral compromise

- worldly habits

- carnal thinking

- mixed worship

- false doctrine

- lukewarm lifestyle

The fear of the Lord creates a clean break.

Compromise is impossible

for a heart that trembles at His Word.

3. BABYLON IS BUILT ON SELF — BUT THE REMNANT IS BUILT ON FEAR

Babylon says:

*   "Follow your feelings."

*   "Follow your desires."

*   "Do what feels right."

*   "Be your own truth."

*   "Worship without holiness."

*   "Serve God on your own terms."

*   "God loves you — no need to repent."

The remnant says:

*   "Not my will, but Yours be done."

*   "Holiness unto the Lord."

*   "Your Word is truth, not my feelings."

*   "I tremble at Your commands."

*   "Your presence is more important than my comfort."

Fear dethrones self.

Fear enthrones God.

4. THE FEAR OF THE LORD MAKES THE REMNANT UNMOVED BY WORLDLY PRESSURE

Babylon pressures you to:

- blend in

- conform

- fit in

- compromise

- be silent

- tolerate sin

- accept ungodly laws

- bow to cultural trends

- embrace spiritual mixture

But the remnant is unmovable.

Psalm 112:7

> *"He will not be afraid of evil tidings;*
> *his heart is steadfast, trusting in the Lord."*

Fear of God makes you immune to the intimidation of Babylon.

The remnant cannot be bought,

cannot be influenced,

cannot be shaken.

5. THE FEAR OF THE LORD EXPOSES BABYLON'S HIDDEN DECEPTIONS

Babylon deceives through:

- religious traditions

- false prophets

- counterfeit worship

- emotional spirituality

- ear-tickling doctrines

- prosperity obsession

- permissive grace

- supernatural mixture

- political idolatry

Only the fear of the Lord reveals the truth.

Psalm 25:14

> *"The secret of the Lord is with those who fear Him."*

Fear gives:

- discernment

- clarity

- insight

- revelation

- supernatural perception

The remnant can see what others cannot.

6. THE FEAR OF THE LORD PURIFIES THE REMNANT FROM BABYLON'S IMMORALITY

Revelation 17 says Babylon is full of:

- fornication

- adultery

- lust

- sexual perversion

- unclean spirits

- sensual worship

This spirit permeates:

- media

- music

- culture

- entertainment

- even the Church

But the remnant walks in:

- purity

- holiness

- modesty

- consecration

- clean thoughts

- clean desires

- clean relationships

Because the fear of the Lord purifies the inner man.

7. THE FEAR OF THE LORD MAKES THE REMNANT REJECT BABYLON'S FALSE UNITY

Babylon offers unity without holiness.

A "come together" movement that sacrifices:

- truth

- holiness

- Scripture

- repentance

- righteousness

It is the unity of compromise,

not the unity of the Spirit.

The remnant cannot unite with Babylon

because fear separates them.

They are united only to:

- Jesus

- His Word

- His truth

- His holiness

- His Spirit

8. THE FEAR OF THE LORD CAUSES THE REMNANT TO ESCAPE BABYLON'S FINAL JUDGMENT

Revelation 18 :8

"Her plagues will come in one day..."

Judgment falls:

- swiftly

- suddenly

- unexpectedly

But not on the remnant.

Why ?

Because they obeyed the command:

"Come out of her, My people."

Fear enables obedience.

Obedience enables escape.

The remnant escapes BOTH:

- Babylon's sins

- Babylon's plagues

Fear saves them from wrath.

9. THE FEAR OF THE LORD TRANSFORMS THE REMNANT INTO A COUNTER-CULTURE

Babylon represents:

- pride

- greed

- immorality

- idolatry

- rebellion

- entertainment

- witchcraft

- luxury

- ego

The remnant embodies:

- humility

- contentment

- holiness

- worship

- obedience

- sobriety

- purity

- simplicity

- Christ-likeness

Fear creates a kingdom culture that confronts Babylon.

10. THE REMNANT STANDS AGAINST BABYLON UNTIL THE KING DESTROYS IT

Revelation 18:21

"Thus, with violence the great city Babylon shall be thrown down..."

Who stands before her destruction?

The remnant.

What sustains them until the end?

The fear of the Lord.

The remnant is the final witness

against Babylon's rebellion.

Their holiness testifies.

Their purity exposes.

Their separation condemns.

Their endurance validates.

Their fear empowers.

They stand until the King arrives.

CLOSING PRAYE

Holy Father,

separate me completely from Babylon.

Break every seductive influence,

every compromise,

every deception,

and every worldly attachment.

Fill me with the fear of the Lord

so, I can see clearly,

discern rightly,

and walk purely in these last days.

Make me a vessel untouched by Babylon,

a witness against darkness,

and a remnant believer who stands

until the fall of this world's systems.

In Jesus' mighty name, Amen.

CHAPTER NINETEEN: THE FEAR OF THE LORD AND THE FINAL MARK OF THE REMNANT: THE SEAL OF GOD

Blueprint of the Remnant, Part IX

Psalm 19:9 — "The fear of the Lord is clean, enduring forever…"

In the last days, the world will be divided into two groups:

- Those marked by the Beast

- Those sealed by God

Revelation 7 reveals a group that will stand untouched by judgment, protected from deception, preserved from wrath, and empowered for the final harvest.

This group is the sealed remnant.

Their mark is not on the hand or forehead—

but on the heart and spirit.

What qualifies them?

The fear of the Lord.

This chapter reveals the deepest mystery of all:

how the fear of God becomes the seal of God on the remnant.

Let's go deeper.

1. THE FEAR OF THE LORD IS WHAT QUALIFIES THE REMNANT TO BE SEALED

Revelation 7:3

"Do not harm the earth... till we have sealed the servants of our God on their foreheads."

Forehead represents:

- the mind

- the thoughts

- the convictions

- the conscience

- the worldview

Why are they sealed?

Because their minds are governed by the fear of God.

Fear:

- shapes their decisions

- filters their thoughts

- governs their conscience

- directs their desires

- orders their steps

The seal of God rests only on those who fear Him.

2. THE FEAR OF THE LORD MAKES THE REMNANT UNMARKABLE BY THE BEAST

Revelation 13 speaks of the mark of the Beast:

- control

- compromise

- worship

- allegiance

- loyalty

- submission to darkness

But the remnant is UNMARKABLE because:

- they fear God

- they reject darkness

- they cannot bow

- they cannot surrender

- they cannot deny Christ

- they cannot compromise

- they cannot be seduced

- they cannot be owned by the world

The fear of the Lord immunizes the remnant from:

- deception

- pressure

- fear of death

- spiritual seduction

- earthly threats

Those who fear God cannot fear the Beast.

3. THE FEAR OF THE LORD PRODUCES UNBREAKABLE LOYALTY

Revelation 14:4

"These are the ones who follow the Lamb wherever He goes."

They follow:

- in persecution

- in wilderness

- in rejection

- in danger

- in poverty

- in suffering

- in isolation

- in testing

Fear produces loyalty.

Loyalty produces the seal.

The seal marks the loyal.

The remnant's devotion is unshakeable because fear governs their hearts.

4. THE FEAR OF THE LORD MAKES THE REMNANT BLAMELESS

Revelation 14:5

> *"In their mouth was found no deceit,*
> *for they are without fault..."*

Blamelessness is not sinlessness—

it is purity of:

- motive

- speech

- heart

- desire

- intention

Fear cleans the inward man.

God seals those who have:

- clean lips

- clean motives

- clean hearts

The remnant's purity becomes their divine mark.

5. THE FEAR OF THE LORD MARKS THE REMNANT WITH GOD'S NAME

Revelation 14:1

"…having His Father's name written on their foreheads."

God's name represents:

- identity

- ownership

- authority

- covering

- covenant

Fear prepares the mind to carry His name.

A mind that fears God carries:

- His thoughts

- His will

- His perspective

- His wisdom

- His convictions

The remnant is marked with God because they fear God.

6. THE FEAR OF THE LORD LEADS TO INNER SEALING BY THE HOLY SPIRIT

Ephesians 1:13

"Having believed, you were sealed with the Holy Spirit of promise."

This sealing is not external.

It is internal.

The Spirit seals the remnant through:

- obedience

- holiness

- repentance

- surrender

- fear

Fear opens the heart wide enough

for God to impress His nature upon it.

Fear is the substance the Holy Spirit seals.

7. THE FEAR OF THE LORD PRODUCES SPIRITUAL RESILIENCE

Revelation 12:11

"They did not love their lives to the death."

What makes a believer able to stand:

- when threatened?

- when persecuted?

- when losing everything?

- when facing death?

Fear of God.

Fear makes suffering small.

Fear makes death powerless.

Fear makes the world worthless.

This is the final mark:

A remnant who cannot be broken.

8. THE FEAR OF THE LORD MAKES THE REMNANT WORSHIPERS IN TRUTH

Revelation 15:4

"Who shall not fear You, O Lord, and glorify Your name?"

The remnant worships because they fear.

They glorify because they tremble.

Worship is not emotional.

It is obedience.

It is purity.

It is holiness.

It is devotion.

It is surrender.

Fear produces true worship.

True worship marks the remnant.

9. THE FEAR OF THE LORD IS THE REMNANT'S PROTECTION DURING JUDGMENT

Revelation 9:4

"...but only those men who do not have the seal of God."

This means:

Those with the seal are protected.

Judgments in Revelation do NOT touch:

- the sealed

- the remnant

- those who fear God

Fear becomes a shield:

- from deception

- from destruction

- from wrath

- from plagues

- from spiritual death

Fear marks the survivors.

Fear marks the protected.

10. THE FEAR OF THE LORD WILL IDENTIFY THE REMNANT BEFORE THE RETURN OF JESUS

By the time the King appears,

the remnant will be known by ONE primary feature:

They fear the Lord more than anything else.

Not their gifting.

Not their charisma.

Not their influence.

Not their ministry.

Not their miracles.

Not their titles.

Their fear.

Fear is their identity.

Fear is their mark.

Fear is their seal.

Fear is their distinction.

Fear is their preservation.

Fear is their covering.

This is God's final mark on His people.

CLOSING PRAYER

Holy Father,

mark me with Your seal.

Print Your name on my mind,

Your Word on my heart,

Your fear in my bones.

Remove every influence of Babylon,

every deception of the Beast,

every compromise of the flesh.

Make me unmarkable by darkness

and unbreakable in persecution.

Seal me with Your presence,

Your truth,

Your holiness,

and Your fear.

In Jesus' mighty name, Amen.

CHAPTER TWENTY: THE FINAL CRY TO THE END-TIME CHURCH: RETURN TO THE FEAR OF THE LORD

Blueprint of the Remnant, Part X — The Final Summoning

Psalm 19:9 — "The fear of the Lord is clean, enduring forever…"

This is the final cry.

The final warning.

The final trumpet.

The final call of God to His people in the last hour.

Return to the Fear of the Lord.

Before the shaking intensifies,

before the judgments increase,

before the Antichrist rises,

before Babylon collapses,

before persecution spreads,

before the final harvest begins,

before the heavens open

and the King returns—

God is calling His Church back to the fear of the Lord.

Not a suggestion.

Not an option.

Not a theological concept.

A CRY from the throne.

This chapter is that cry.

Let us go deeper.

1. THE CHURCH IS DYING BECAUSE IT LOST THE FEAR OF THE LORD

In many places today:

- sin is tolerated

- holiness is mocked

- compromise is justified

- pulpits are powerless

- truth is softened

- repentance is neglected

- worship is entertainment

- leaders fall morally with no trembling

- people live however they want

- the world enters the church instead of the church entering the world

Why?

Because the fear of God is gone.

No fear → no holiness.

No fear → no power.

No fear → no presence.

No fear → no conviction.

No fear → no glory.

No fear → no true worship.

No fear → no revival.

No fear → no remnant.

The Church has become familiar with God,

casual with God,

irreverent toward God.

The result?

Spiritual death.

2. GOD IS CALLING HIS PEOPLE TO RETURN TO HOLY FEAR

Revelation 2:5

"Remember… repent… and do the first works."

The first work is fear.

Fear is where obedience begins.

Fear is where holiness begins.

Fear is where wisdom begins.

Fear is where intimacy begins.

Fear is where union begins.

Fear is where revival begins.

The Spirit is crying:

"Return to trembling."

"Return to reverence."

"Return to holiness."

"Return to purity."

"Return to brokenness."

"Return to Me."

3. THE FINAL GENERATION MUST BE GOVERNED BY THE FEAR OF GOD

Isaiah 33:6

"…the fear of the Lord is His treasure."

In the last days, the fear of the Lord will be the Church's greatest treasure:

- not money

- not buildings

- not programs

- not crowds

- not entertainment

- not positions

- not titles

- not talent

But fear.

Fear will be the foundation of the end-time Church.

Fear will be the standard of the end-time remnant.

Fear will be the identity of the end-time Bride.

Fear will be the defense of the end-time army.

Fear is the treasure.

4. THE CHURCH MUST CHOOSE BETWEEN FEAR OF GOD OR FEAR OF MAN

Matthew 10:28

> *"Do not fear those who kill the body...*
> *but fear Him who is able to destroy both soul and body in hell."*

The final battle will expose:

- who fears God

- who fears man

- who fears death

- who fears rejection

- who fears losing comfort

- who fears losing reputation

Only those who fear God will remain standing.

The Church must choose now—

before the shaking intensifies.

5. GOD IS CALLING LEADERS BACK TO THE FEAR OF THE LORD

Ezekiel 44:23

> *"They shall teach My people the difference between the holy and the unholy."*

Leaders must:

- stop entertaining

- stop compromising

- stop sugarcoating truth

- stop twisting Scripture

- stop justifying sin

- stop prioritizing crowds over holiness

- stop preaching a God they themselves don't fear

God is raising up leaders who tremble before Him—

leaders who fear no man but the Holy One.

Men and women of holy fear will shepherd the remnant Church.

6. GOD IS CALLING THE NATIONS TO FEAR HIM BEFORE JUDGMENT FALLS

Revelation 14:7

*"Fear God and give glory to Him,
for the hour of His judgment has come."*

Before judgment, God gives mercy.

Before wrath, God sends warning.

Before destruction, God sends prophets.

The final warning is simple:

FEAR GOD.

Without fear, nations collapse.

Without fear, morality decays.

Without fear, darkness increases.

Without fear, judgment becomes inevitable.

Fear is the last call to mercy.

7. THE FEAR OF THE LORD IS THE ONLY SAFE PLACE IN THE FINAL HOUR

Proverbs 14:26

*"In the fear of the Lord is strong confidence,
and His children shall have a place of refuge."*

Refuge is not found in:

- governments

- medicine

- politics

- money

- systems

- alliances

- denominations

- security plans

Refuge is found in the fear of the Lord alone.

Fear is the shelter.

Fear is the covering.

Fear is the protection.

The remnant will survive because they fear.

8. GOD IS RAISING UP A REMNANT WHO WILL RESTORE FEAR TO THE CHURCH

Joel 2:1

"Blow the trumpet in Zion..."

This is the trumpet call:

Restore the fear of God.

The remnant will preach fear.

The remnant will live fear.

The remnant will model fear.

The remnant will carry fear.

The remnant will produce fear in others.

The remnant will reintroduce fear to a dying Church.

This book is part of that trumpet.

9. FEAR OF THE LORD WILL SEPARATE THE TRUE CHURCH FROM THE FALSE

In the last days, there will be:

- a harlot church (Babylon)

- a remnant Church (Zion)

One is religious.

One is holy.

One is compromised.

One is consecrated.

One loves the world.

One fears the Lord.

Fear is the dividing line.

Those who fear God are the true Church.

Those who do not fear God—even if they attend church—are not.

10. THE FINAL CALL: RETURN TO FEAR, RETURN TO HOLINESS, RETURN TO GOD

This is the cry of the Spirit in these last days:

Return.

Repent.

Tremble again.

Seek again.

Surrender again.

Yield again.

Pursue again.

Obey again.

Love again.

Fear again.

This is not a suggestion.

This is a summons from the throne of God.

The time is short.

The hour is late.

The shaking is near.

The glory is coming.

The King is standing at the door.

Return to the fear of the Lord—

before it is too late.

FINAL PRAYER — A CRY FOR FEAR, HOLINESS, AND READINESS

Holy Father,

restore to me the fear of the Lord.

Break every hardness in my heart,

every compromise in my life,

every distraction in my soul.

Bring me back to trembling,

back to reverence,

back to holiness,

back to surrender,

back to purity,

back to obedience.

Make me part of the remnant

that fears Your name,

loves Your presence,

keeps Your Word,

and remains faithful to the end.

Mark me, refine me, separate me,

prepare me for the coming of the King.

Lord Jesus,

I return to the fear of the Lord.

Amen.

FINAL PRAYER OF THE BOOK:
A CRY FOR THE FEAR OF THE LORD TO RETURN TO THE CHURCH

Psalm 19:9 — "The fear of the Lord is clean, enduring forever…"

Holy and Righteous Father,

We come before You with trembling hearts,

knowing that You are great,

You are holy,

You are majestic,

and You are to be feared above all gods.

We acknowledge, Lord,

that the Church in this generation has drifted—

drifted into comfort,

drifted into compromise,

drifted into worldliness,

drifted into religion without power,

drifted into worship without holiness,

drifted into ministry without surrender,

drifted into confession without repentance.

But today, O God,

we hear Your voice calling us back—

back to the old paths,

back to holiness,

back to reverence,

back to purity,

back to truth,

back to full surrender,

back to the fear of the Lord.

Father, restore Your fear in us.

Let it break our pride.

Let it crush our idols.

Let it cleanse our motives.

Let it purify our desires.

Let it sanctify our hearts.

Let it transform our minds.

Let it awaken our spirits.

Create in us a heart that trembles at Your Word.

Give us ears that heed Your warnings.

Give us eyes that see through deception.

Give us a conscience sensitive to Your Spirit.

Give us a will fully surrendered to Your commands.

Lord Jesus,

You are the King of glory,

the Judge of all the earth,

the Lamb who was slain,

the Lion who is returning.

Prepare Your Bride.

Purify Your people.

Refine Your remnant.

Cleanse Your Church.

Let Your fear fall again—

in our homes,

in our churches,

in our pulpits,

in our gatherings,

in our worship,

in our decisions,

in our daily lives.

Let holy fear grip our leaders.

Let holy fear shake our congregations.

Let holy fear burn in our youth.

Let holy fear awaken our families.

Let holy fear drive us back to repentance.

Lord, make us again a people of conviction—

a people who stand for righteousness,

a people who refuse compromise,

a people who embrace holiness,

a people who honor Your presence,

a people who love truth

more than comfort,

more than popularity,

more than approval.

Baptize us in the Spirit of the Fear of the Lord.

Mark us with Your seal.

Strengthen us as Your remnant.

Prepare us for the final hour.

Make us faithful until the end,

so that when You come,

You will find a Bride

who is ready,

pure,

holy,

and filled with oil.

Father, we cry out—

Let the fear of the Lord return to the Church.

Let the fear of the Lord return to the nations.

Let the fear of the Lord return to the earth.

Let the fear of the Lord return to our hearts.

For Yours is the kingdom,

and the power,

and the glory,

forever and ever.

In the mighty, holy, and precious name of Jesus Christ—

Amen and Amen.

CLOSING REFLECTION: A FINAL CALL TO YOUR HEART

"The fear of the Lord is clean, enduring forever." — Psalm 19:9

You have reached the end of this book—

but not the end of God's call.

This is not a conclusion.

This is an invitation.

A divine invitation to return to the place where everything begins:

the fear of the Lord.

As you reflect on what you have read,

take a moment—right now—

to quiet your heart before God.

Lay aside distractions.

Lay aside the noise of your day.

Lay aside every other voice.

And ask yourself:

- Do I truly fear the Lord?

- Does my life reflect His holiness?

- Is my heart clean before Him?

- Are there areas of compromise I've overlooked?

- Do I tremble at His Word?

- Have I allowed the world to dull my reverence?

- Am I prepared to stand in the final hour?

- Am I walking as part of the remnant?

These are not questions of condemnation.

They are questions of awakening—

questions of mercy—

questions of love.

The Holy Spirit is not pointing a finger of accusation.

He is extending a hand of restoration.

The fear of the Lord is not meant to push you away from God—

it is meant to draw you deeper into Him.

It is the doorway to:

- intimacy

- purity

- revelation

- strength

- holiness

- protection

- power

- true worship

- true repentance

- true transformation

The fear of the Lord is not just a doctrine;

it is a lifestyle.

It is a posture.

It is a heart condition.

It is a covenant between you and God.

It is the foundation on which every other aspect of your walk must be built.

This entire book has been a cry—

a cry to you,

a cry to the Church,

a cry to the nations,

a cry to the remnant,

a cry to the Bride.

But now the cry must become your personal response.

You have a choice.

You can put this book down and move on with life as usual.

Or you can decide—today—

that you will live differently.

Walk differently.

Pray differently.

Worship differently.

Obey differently.

Love differently.

Serve differently.

Think differently.

Fear God differently.

This is your moment

to return to the ancient path.

To take up the mantle of holiness.

To walk in the footsteps of the remnant.

To embrace the call of God for this generation.

To stand as a light in a darkened world.

To become one of the few

who truly fear the Lord.

Let this final reflection be your personal covenant:

"Lord, I return to the fear of the Lord.

I return to holiness.

I return to purity.

I return to Your presence.

I return to trembling at Your Word.

I return to the path of obedience.

I return to You."

This is the moment heaven is waiting for.

This is the moment your spirit has longed for.

This is the moment that shifts your future.

Now, let the fear of the Lord

be the atmosphere of your heart.

Let it guard your steps.

Let it shape your decisions.

Let it purify your motives.

Let it awaken your spirit.

Let it prepare you for the return of the King.

Because when everything else fades—

when kingdoms fall,

when systems collapse,

when the world shakes,

when darkness rises—

the fear of the Lord endures forever.

And those who walk in it

will stand forever.